THE ART OF THE THEATRE

THE ART OF THE
THEATRE

BY

SARAH BERNHARDT

TRANSLATED BY H. J. STENNING

WITH A PREFACE BY JAMES AGATE

Select Bibliographies Reprint Series

BOOKS FOR LIBRARIES PRESS
FREEPORT, NEW YORK

First Published 1924
Reprinted 1969

STANDARD BOOK NUMBER:
8369-5038-0

LIBRARY OF CONGRESS CATALOG CARD NUMBER:
77-94265

PRINTED IN THE UNITED STATES OF AMERICA

Preface

WHEN Mr. Bles invited me to write a short preface to this book my first instinct was to refuse. A *short* preface? *Ah, mais non!* One might use all the words in two languages and then fail to do justice to that world-figure, but the attempt would not have lacked scope. And then it occurred to me that what I was asked to provide was not a full-length portrait, nor even any portrait at all, but a simple appreciation of the last workings of that busy brain which only death could still. But surely this demand is more exorbitant than that other would have been. It is almost impossible to write a little about Bernhardt. The whole mountain, if you like, but not the lower slopes.

Yet how ineffectual that major task! Sarah is at once spur and knell to those who would hand her down the ages. Her memory is a spiritual tyranny: all who knew her are conscious that we owe a remembrancer to posterity, and know, too, that our words are futile.

> " Et, pour que le néant ne touche point à lui,
> C'est assez d'un enfant sur sa mère endormi."

Raphael is still Raphael ; Bernhardt is no more. It is an old story, this evanescence of the stage-artist, and I see some decline of poetry in that Musset's *Stances à la Malibran* have found no echo in these later days.

No echo in verse, it were perhaps better to say. For some of us, whose duty it is to chronicle the trespasses as well as the triumphs of the scene, have decked out our poor prose to a semblance of the radiance which is gone. By some irony the writer who has done most nobly by that great memory is not a dramatic critic but a man of letters who still regards the drama as part of the province of literature. Mr. Maurice Baring begins what may very well become the last word upon Sarah Bernhardt with the first line of Musset's poem—" *Sans doute il est trop tard pour parler encor d'elle.*" He makes—and was bound to make—the old point that there can be no such thing as a reconstruction of a dead artist. Threnody is all. Cinematograph films revealing her gestures are nothing. Gramophones recording a " poor

ghost of her voice " are nothing. For Bernhardt's art, Mr. Baring tells us, was a complex
whole made up of rhythmical movement, gesture,
look, speech, hands, hair, body and spirit. And
then these beautiful words follow : " Those who
never saw her will only be able to guess at it
(Bernhardt's art), but it will be one of the beautiful and permanent guesses of mankind." Later
Mr. Baring has his majestic close, as we all must
on taking leave of her whom we have more than
loved. Homer and Phidias, he tells us, are after
all but as flotsam drifting for a little while upon
the stream of Time. Then comes the concluding
phrase. " And with it now there is a strange
russet leaf, the name of Sarah Bernhardt."
" Russet " is a beautiful word, used here most
exquisitely, but it is also a literary word. And
I keep the best of my admiration for the simpler
" one of the beautiful and permanent guesses
of mankind."

But I must, I suppose, leave Sarah, and come
to her work. My own liveliest recollection of
the writer attaches to that November day when
she took luncheon at my mother's house in the
outskirts of Manchester. This was a red-
letter day in the annals of my family, and I
have described it elsewhere. More to the point
here would be some account of a lesson which

I once saw and heard her give to a class of pupils on the stage of her theatre in Paris. This must have been, I suppose, some three or four years prior to the war ; and my sister, who was afterwards to act with Sarah for some three or four years, was at that time a member of the class. A rostrum, screened from the draughts, was erected in the place where the prompter's box usually appears. The pupils, nearly all young girls, though here and there an actress with a foot on a lower rung of the professional ladder, sat round the back of the stage in a semicircle. There was something of the whispering hush of an excited congregation. And then Sarah appeared. She wore that mantle known to every photographer in Europe, and to me recalling the misty breasts of sea-birds. She was supported by a devoted secretary and a woman friend, and her entry was not unlike that which she used for the third act of *Phèdre*.

And here my recollection plays the traitor, loitering among trivialities unworthy to be recorded. Can it, I wonder, be of interest that the great actress drank a glass of milk and refreshed herself by sniffing the perfumes of ten or a dozen handkerchiefs which she kept on the desk before her ? I remember that some American Sadie or Mamie, glittering with

diamonds, endeavoured to take Sarah by rhe-
torical storm, and was accorded a frigid " *Vous
avez fait du progrès, mademoiselle ! Continuez !* "
But to a plain and clever girl, who had obviously
given time and thought to a long passage
from Racine's *Bérénice*, Sarah gave her most
earnest attention. She did nothing but scold,
and to be scolded by Sarah was an indication
that the pupil possessed within her at least the
seeds of acting.

Perhaps an anecdote may not be out of place.
The plain girl was succeeded by a little waif
who was making a study of the distressed heroines
of melodrama. " *Au secours !* " she lisped,
in a voice which could not have been heard
beyond the first row of stalls. In vain was she
exhorted to more desperate effort, and at last
her twitterings broke down in tears.

" Won't you say it for me, Madame," she
sobbed, " and then perhaps . . . ? "

" My child," Sarah replied, " regard me then
those workmen painting the ceiling. If I were
to cry for help they would come rushing down
on to the stage, and I pay them by the hour ! "

This little book contains many of those hints
upon the art of acting which I was too careless
or too idle to record on that afternoon of long
ago. It is put together carelessly. But then

did not Death catch the artist as Montaigne
decided that it should catch him, " whilest I am
setting my cabiges, carelesse of her darte. . . ."
The order of the thoughts in this little volume
is undisciplined, but the thoughts themselves
are those of a sensible, disciplined mind.
For Sarah was as sensible a woman as ever
lived, as stern of purpose as Florence Nightin-
gale, as matter-of-fact as Mrs. Humphry Ward.
For sixty years she worked like a horse, and in
the end she came to possess a large amount of
something very like horse-sense. This book
is to be studied by the beginner and also by the
player of genius.

"*Apportez le fatras, chérie!*" she would
say to Mme. Normand, when she had half an
hour to spare. And the phrase has the ring of
Sarah's essential simplicity.

JAMES AGATE.

Contents

	PAGE
INTRODUCTION BY M. MARCEL BERGER . . .	13
FIRST HINTS	19
THE THEATRE	27

FIRST PART

THE PHYSICAL QUALITIES NECESSARY TO THE ACTOR

THE MEMORY	37
PHYSICAL PROPORTIONS	42
THE VOICE	50
PRONUNCIATION	62
GESTURE	79

SECOND PART

THE MORAL QUALITIES NECESSARY TO THE ACTOR

THE ACTOR'S RÔLE	83
INSTRUCTION	87
THE CHOICE OF A PART	91
THE WILL	93
NATURALISM	98
SENSIBILITY	101

11

12 *Contents*

THIRD PART

IMPRESSIONS—CRITICISMS—MEMORIES

		PAGE
POETRY	. . . .	109
WHY I COULD NOT PLAY CORNEILLE	. . .	125
WHY I HAVE PLAYED MALE PARTS	. . .	137
THE ACTOR AND THE PUBLIC	. . . .	145
MISCELLANEOUS HINTS	. . . . .	165
THE INFLUENCE OF THE THEATRE	. . .	174
OUR ART	. . . .	189

APPENDIX

| HINTS ON MAKING-UP | . . . . . | 213 |
| HINTS ON THE VOICE | . . . . . | 218 |

Introduction

" I AM incurably young," she said, with a smile that was not without a trace of sadness.

Although over seventy-five, she overflowed with energy, vitality, and sprightliness. Why did she take up writing with such enthusiasm so late in life ? It was not for need of money, when her appearance in *Daniel* and in *Athalie* filled immense theatres with an adoring crowd, which poured its money into the box-office.

" To amuse myself."

" To amuse herself," she tirelessly dictated those tales of bizarre tenderness, those sentimental novels relieved by flashes of humour, of which the readers of the *Annales* and of the *Gaulois*, if I may judge from the number of letters received, grew passionately fond.

And then one day—it was in the spring of 1920 —she finished *Petite Idole*.

" It is not entirely a question of amusing myself," she told me. " I must try to be useful. I have had at least a little experience, which has been pretty dearly bought. There is advice that I should like to give beginners, especially as scarcely any was given me. I have not thought things out so badly, although I am by no means a philosopher. But concerning the theatre, its rules, its incidental interests, its glorious authors and artists, its great repertory works, as well as its contemporary plays, there are things that I feel . . . that I feel . . ."

She put her hand on her heart.

" Do you think this would make a book ? "

Together we discussed the form it should take. She fingered the excellent treatise of Melchissédec.

" Oh no, I should never be able to write according to a fixed design."

" Very well," I said, " dictate chapters upon questions which attract you, no matter in what order, and then we will try to fit the ' puzzle ' together."

From then onwards, whenever she had a free hour, she would summon her secretary and dictate.

Imagine the life she led, a woman mortally ill, obliged to take incessant precautions, with plays to read, the lectures to prepare, her novels, her scenarios, from which she would never omit a line, her journeys, her business cares, visits from intimate friends or from the many world celebrities

visiting Paris !   This was the usual routine.   In
her free hours, I say, she would summon her secretary, at one time Mademoiselle Gourjon, latterly
Madame Normand.

"Come let us attend to serious matters !" she
would say.

The most important of these was this book.   I
would hear her dictating it with her voice often
radiantly clear, sometimes slightly dim, but regain-
ing its unique timbre the moment it passed the
splendid barrier of her teeth.

She would throw off the title of a chapter and
sketch the development of an argument.   Then a
chance memory or anecdote would cause a digres-
sion.   In three lines she would sketch a picture,
a feature, or a portrait with that gift for caricature
which was one of her characteristics.   The secretary would pause, out-distanced by the narrator,
or raise her eyes, astonished at the acute criticism.

Sarah would laugh :

"No, not that dear !   There are quite enough
people who detest me already !   We cannot write
this down.   If X were here, I should tell him so
to his face, and perhaps we should become good
friends."

The chapter ended, which often had only a very
slender connection with its title, she would have it
read back to her, and she would correct and amend

with an undeniable sense of composition and style. Some phrase would disquiet her.

" Can one say that ?   Is it French ? "

We would then look it up in *Littré*.   And often she would retort :

" So much the worse.   We can't all be grammarians."

Thus during three years, and chiefly during her summer months at Belle-Isle, the material of the present book gradually took shape.   In October of last year she was about to leave for her Italian tour, which turned out such a triumph.   She spoke to me of Mussolini, whom she admired, and who, I told her, would ask to be introduced to her, and of America, whither she hoped so much to return :

" They are the greatest people !   They showed this during the war.   Terrible when it was necessary ; and then the first to talk of peace.   Fifteen years ago they were still sympathetic barbarians ; to-day they are catching us up in refinement and in courtesy.   I should like to tell them again that I love them."

There was further discussion about Sacha Guitry, whose *Roman d'Amour* she was beginning to rehearse, about Maurice (Maurice Rostand) whom she loved like a spoilt child.   At the end of the *déjeuner*, before departing for her theatre, where she was due to rehearse at three o'clock :

" Bring in all that litter, dear," she said to Madame Normand.

It was indeed a litter ; there were about five hundred pages in large writing.

" The task is finished," she informed me. " Now it has to be polished up. I have given some thought to it."

She showed me, written with her own hand on a small sheet of paper, these words :

1. Physical Qualities.
2. Moral Qualities.
3. Memories and Impressions.

On her return from Italy we were to arrange another meeting, in order to collate this pile of notes and put the whole in order, deleting repetitions and cutting out redundancies.

Alas, the crisis of blood poisoning had already supervened when in March I had my last interview with the dying woman, about to surrender her ardent love of life. Lying on a couch that was decked and cold as the couch of a corpse, she said to me, pushing the faded blossoms aside :

" And ' The Art of the Theatre,' my friend, I rely on you to arrange for that . . ."

It was with a heavy heart that I returned to the Boulevard Pereire, to the confusion of a dwelling that was dusty and dead. Madame Normand

and I perused the heap of papers, collected with pious solicitude by M. Maurice Bernhardt.

I carried away the " litter," the very name of which brought tears to my eyes. It was swollen by many pages, by scribbled notes, written either by the illustrious artist or by her secretaries, and some of these had already been used for certain lectures, or for a particular fragment of her *Mémoires*.

It was an ungrateful and considerable task, but it did not exceed the resources of my courage and of my affection. M. Georges Ribemont-Dessaignes, whose curious essays had so much interested Sarah Bernhardt in recent years, assisted me with all his perspicacity. We divided the chapters and collated the notes ; with a discreet pen we sketched some transitions ; perhaps now and again we re-touched some phrase, but never when the original text reflected the individuality of the glorious artist whom we mourned.

And here is the book. Doubtless you will miss the closely-woven texture of certain treatises by professional writers, but you will see the great actress alive and speaking of the subject most dear to her, the theatre that she loved, studied, and adorned as the greatest artist in the world. " I feel . . . I feel . . ." she had said. This book did indeed spring from her heart.

MARCEL BERGER.

First Hints

I HAVE not written this book to attract young people to the dramatic art, but to give them friendly advice, and guide them by my experience.

I have now followed my profession for more than sixty years, and the public has shown me favour ever since my first appearance. I have recollected all the studies that I have added to my natural gifts, and take pleasure in preparing a firm stirrup for those neophytes who wish to mount Pegasus, the steed of Aurora and the Muses.

I would warn young people against all those ideas of brilliance, mirth, and flattery which are suggested by our art. How many charming but mediocre people have I seen floundering in the mud of the stage, how many pure young girls lost for ever through compromising situations veiled by hope. Poor little victims, so easy to catch in the clumsiest trap, and for whom the poachers of love who hover around theatres have no pity at all.

Alas, in the dramatic art many are called, but few are chosen ; to be sure all the chosen are not of the same degree ; among them are stars that shine with a more effulgent light than others. But in the artistic firmament there can only be stars and lesser luminaries, nothing else.

You who only see the bright side of our art, that is success and popularity ; you who have only entered the large fashionable drawing-room, where move ladies in beautiful dresses, loaded with diamonds or pearls, or the ducal palace of a fifteenth century grandee, in which the finest brocades rustle at each movement of an elegant patrician as she is saluted by a crowd of nobles ; you who have heard the words issuing from the heroine's lips as lightly as a flight of white butter-flies (for only white butterflies are really volatile) ; you who have seen all this from your stall on a first night, in the brilliant atmosphere of intellectuals ; you who have trembled and wept ; you who have feverishly clapped your hands to express your grateful admiration ; you who have seen all this, give me your hand and come with me.

It is half an hour after noon. You cannot see where you are ? Why, you are in the same draw-ing-room that you saw yesterday evening. You can't see, you say ? Oh, to be sure, in the morn-ing the saloon is only lighted by this little globe hanging from a wire.   It is called the *servante* and also the *Baladeuse*.

" But what is going on at this moment ? " you ask.

" They are making a slight adjustment, because the actress who played the young American lady has become hoarse, and has to be replaced."

" Oh ! my foot is in a hole."

" No, it is a groove ; one often twists one's ankle in it.   Fortunately this hasn't happened to you, but move carefully."

" Ah ! my foot is free, but my heel is stuck in the groove."

" Yes, one wants Louis XV heels made by the great bootmaker."

" Ah ! yes, but good heavens, what a bad smell, Madame ! "

" Yes, all theatres have a bad smell."

" Oh ! but it seemed to me that it smelt sweet enough when the curtain went up last night."

" And you are right, the actresses use a lot of scent in the evening."

" Who are those shabby people sitting in a ring ? "

" They are the dukes, duchesses, princes, princesses, and other ladies and gentlemen who thronged the saloon yesterday evening, during the festivities in the fourth act."

" In God's name, who is that leaning on the column ; the whole background has been pitched down," shouts a rough voice.

" Have you hurt yourself, Mademoiselle ? "

" Not that I know of.   I seemed to be feeling giddy and leaned against the column, which gave way.   Yesterday it supported a large basket of fresh flowers, so it must be heavy."

" No, my young friend, it is only painted canvas and it supports only painted flowers ; in the evening there is one in the foreground which is made of real marble and supports a real basket of flowers.   But the theatre, like life, has several aspects ; one must only rely on the real which is the foreground of life, and beware of the others which are unreal.   Since you have done nothing amiss and have only one heel, sit down here and listen."

" Who is the gentleman approaching us ? "

" That is the second manager.   It is he who uttered those rough words you heard."

" What a horrid man ! "

" Yes, but there are many worse.   Good morning, Benoit."

" Oh ! Madame, I did not know you were there !   Pardon me."

" Since you know how to control yourself when I am here, which is nearly always, you have no excuse, and you are very coarse.   Go on with the rehearsal without revealing my presence."

"Why does the lady rehearsing the part of the American girl speak like that ?"

"She is mumbling her words in order to have more control over herself."

"But why is M. Benoit abusing her so.   It is a shame.   Poor girl.   Look ! she is weeping."

"Come away ! I do not want her to know that I'm here.   That would make it all too serious. It will soon be settled, as everything is settled in the theatre.   Actors are very honest and have a high sense of fairness.   It very rarely happens that any wanton harm is done, or good fellowship jeopardized."

Come, you are already disappointed, and this is only the material side, the ugliness of people and things.   But there is worse to come : such things as moral vexations, intellectual vexations, injustices, the annoyances of tuition, the wretched blackmailing press that drags you in the mud if you have the opportunity to become somebody ; there is the insolence of certain girls against whom you cannot fight, not wanting to make use of the same weapons, and then there is that mysterious something that draws the attention of the public. For want of a better word, this mysterious thing has been called " charm."   You must have this

charm to reach the pinnacle.   It is made of everything and of nothing, the striving will, the look, the
walk, the proportions of the body, the sound of
the voice, the ease of the gestures.   It is not at all
necessary to be handsome or to be pretty ; all that
is needful is charm, the charm that holds the attention of the spectator, so that he listens rapt, and on
leaving seeks to be alone, in order to recapture the
charm he has felt.

However, this charm manifests itself in different
ways.   There is the charm that emanates from a
feline grace made up of pretty movements, the
charm that steals over you through the musical
sound of the voice, the charm wafted from a person
whose soul is clean and loyal, the charm not less
taking of a subtle and elaborate- brain, and the
poetic charm that is the most delusive of all, for it is
only a flimsy armour against the material blemishes
of nature.   Nevertheless, the charm of poetry in
a woman is the most captivating of all.   Then
there is the charm exuded by a healthy and lively
person, and that lasts the shortest time of all.

At the Théâtre Français we used to divide the
public into several categories.   When Croizette
and I were playing together, the public sometimes
fell into two camps, as for instance in the *Sphinx* of
Octave Feuillet, or *l'Étrangère* of Dumas *fils*.

There were the stout bankers, the stout red-faced men, who enjoyed life, these formed the camp of Sophie Croizette ; then there were the poets, the dreamers, the students, the neurasthenic subjects, and the young girls, who represented my camp. And this collection of diverse mentalities fused its admirations into overflowing measure. The feather-brains blushed with pleasure to see and hear Croizette, their replete stomachs rising and falling in ecstasy. They clapped their pudgy hands, and the shouts of " bravo ! splendid ! " quickly winded these worthy men about town. But my long-haired and empty-bellied public started as if electrified, and young hands clapped like whips and young girls threw me flowers ; and all this animation compelled the most reluctant to confound us both in the same success, although it had only been intended to exalt one victor.

The Theatre

THE art of the theatre is the most difficult of all the arts, as I will show. Sculpture, drawing, and painting find in nature all the materials necessary for their embodiment : beasts and human beings. For music there is the keyboard, while literature may draw its vital forces from all society and all classes. It even has the right to steal from history its tragedies and anecdotes. The lives of each and all furnish it with innumerable and fresh canvases, and imagination is its absolute domain.

It is true that the art of the theatre includes all the arts, but it also presupposes the possession of natural gifts, which have to be supplemented by laborious training.

A canvas and brush suffice a painter ; modelling clay, boasting-tool, and chisel are the appropriate implements of the sculptor. A sheet of paper and pen satisfy the writer ; the seven octaves of a piano facilitate the inspiration of the composer, and the apostles of these different arts are at

liberty to be bandy-legged, hump-backed, de-
formed, and even deaf like Beethoven, without
their works suffering from their defects.

The neophytes of the theatrical art must possess
a retentive memory, excellent bodily proportions,
and a fine voice.   These three points are the primordial qualities essential to the future of a great
artist.   In the case of an adult who chooses the
dramatic career, they are advantages that can be
perfected by study.   Still he or she must have had
them from birth.

To these must be added other qualities that are
more easily acquired, such as voice production,
pronunciation, breathing, gesture, and expression.
I do not say, you understand, that a person is a
talented artist because he or she has all these needful things ; not in the least ; this combination of
gifts is merely the spring-board which will serve
as a basis for all the other accomplishments necessary to the portrayal of love, hate, anger, joy,
gentleness, duplicity, candour, wit, and folly.

Among these accomplishments, the art of speaking is the most difficult to acquire, and many
young artists relinquish this study altogether,
which is why great artists are so few.

The Conservatoire is necessary, although it does
not render the services it ought to render to our
French Art.   I must, however, admit that the

first-class artists who honour the theatres with
their talent at this moment are products of the
Conservatoire.   They are only the exceptions who
had in abundant measure the innate advantages
enumerated above.

The general belief is that it is sufficient to be
pretty or to be handsome in order to enter the
theatre, and unfortunately the bad choice of the
jury in the Conservatoire examinations confirms
the ignorant public in this idea.   I have often
heard outsiders say to a mother, in speaking of her
daughter :

" Oh ! how pretty she will look on the stage."

And my eyes lighting on the child would show
me the pretty features of a head that was too big,
and had no neck, supported by a slender little
body, with arms that were too long.   The truth,
the absolute truth, is that the chief beauty for the
theatre consists in fine bodily proportions.

A face that is too large may be corrected by a
wig, which diminishes the area of the cheeks.   A
face that is too long may be wrapped at its base in
tulles or frills.   There have been ugly actresses
who have achieved great triumphs, such as Annie
Desclée, who created *Frou-frou* with resounding
success, and *Frou-frou*, moreover, is a charming
person for whom two men fight each other.   But
Annie Desclée was slender and well-proportioned,

neither big nor little, having a colourless face and
prominent eyes.   After her facial defects had been
rectified by a slight but very skilful touching-up,
she could give the illusion, if not of beauty, at
least of agreeableness.

I want to mention the case of a young girl
who belonged to the upper middle class.   She
was named Mary Julien and made her first
appearance at the Odéon in *Balsamo* by Alexander
Dumas the Great.   I was in a box, and in the
next box was Catulle Mendès.   He had arrived
at the moment the curtain was raised, for he
was one of those critics who are full of professional honesty ;   but having prolonged his
absence after the first act, he did not return until
the middle of the second.

Mary Julien was on the stage, and at the end of
two or three minutes, while she was repeating I
forget which passage of her part, I heard Mendès
say to a friend who was with him :

" But what is she doing kneeling such a long
time ? "

Mary Julien was standing up, but her body was
so long and her legs so short that she gave the
illusion of kneeling.   This semi-deformity prevented her from reaching the position which her
real talent, her magnificent voice, and her pretty
golden-haired head had caused her drawing-room

admirers to predict for her. Like many other actresses of whom the public are ignorant, Mary Julien had begun by shining in drawing-rooms. Ah ! how many of these amiable people of the world are responsible, unconsciously it is true, for broken lives ? It is so very different to listen at close-quarters to a young girl saying verses or a monologue, or playing a little scene. All the defects evaporate in the indifferent, mundane atmosphere ; these amiable guests are not there to judge ; they are there to enjoy themselves, to bestow praise on the artists and thanks on the hosts, and they say and do what politeness demands.

But the young artists take it all quite seriously, the compliments, the applause, the discreet little laughs, or the sighs of suppressed emotion. And there they are, poor children, excited by dreams of the future, which seem to them so splendid that many break the ties of marriage or of the family, in order to plunge into the unknown without any other guide than the false star they have followed.

The majority lose their road and remain in the tortuous labyrinth of hope.

During my short term as a teacher at the Conservatoire, I had an opportunity to observe the vast apathy of the members of the jury. I had in my class a youth possessed of a fine baritone voice, but having a very common appearance, a large head with a very short neck, excessively long arms ending in enormously large hands, and flat feet to match the hands. Why had this youth been admitted ? Mounet Sully answered me :

" My dear friend, he has a magnificent voice."

" I agree, but let him go to the singing class."

After testing all my pupils on the first day of my class, I told this young man that he would make a splendid singer, but would never be anything but an abominable actor. He followed my advice and six months afterwards he passed the singing examination. And two years later he made his first appearance in a large Paris theatre. I must admit that I was glad to continue offering him my advice, since the dramatic art was no longer in question. I also had in a class a rather handsome youth who lisped perceptibly. He went into the cinema where he made his fortune—but why was he allowed into the Conservatoire ?

When a teacher discovers a pupil who is apt to assimilate his pet ideas, he favours him and is unsparing of his support and advice. He is quite satisfied when his pupil carries off the first prize at the competition, which often happens too soon, as the young artist is only superficially prepared, and owes to his natural gifts alone a success which in the majority of cases will not last.

The great mistake of the jury is a neglect to discern those gifts, which may certainly be cultivated, but whose natural existence is essential to the neophyte for the development of his future as tragedian or comedian, and the permanent safety of his career.

FIRST PART

The Physical Qualities necessary to the Actor

The Memory

IT matters little whether the memory be slow, fleeting, retentive, quick, or profound : the dramatic artist must " have a memory." If not, he stammers or waits on the prompter, which is distasteful. Indeed it is only in France that the prompter with his wretched little box is still permitted to spoil the view of the spectator and generally disturb the decorative harmony. The life of the drama is perturbed by the interpreter's shortcomings, his omissions mar the thought of the author and confuse the public. It is not for nothing that Mnemosyne, the mother of the Muses, was the goddess of Memory.

Dame memory is a most worthy person, but she must be cultivated and never neglected. Some memories are very capricious. Mounet Sully remembered verse better than prose. De Max, who has a stubborn memory, visualizes and remembers the directions in turning the pages. Rejane had a memory that was perfect in every way. As for me I need only read a part two or three times, and I know it infallibly ; but the moment I cease to play in the piece, the part slips away from me, carried off by some mysterious current. My memory box cannot contain several parts at the same time, and it is impossible for me to recite haphazard a passage from *Phèdre* or from *Hamlet*. And yet I can remember the most trifling incidents of my earliest infancy.

On one occasion I had a very serious lapse of memory on the stage of which I was not aware at the time. It occurred in London at the Gaiety Theatre. The previous evening I had been ill ; overwork had brought on such a hemorrhage that Doctors Vintras and Parrot refused to let me play in the evening my part in *L'Étrangère* of Alexandre Dumas. I took no notice. The opium which they gave me in a potion left my head a little heavy. I went on the stage, almost unconscious but delighted with the reception I received. I walked in a dream and had difficulty in distinguishing my surroundings. The sound of my voice sounded to me very far away. I was in that delicious stupor that one experiences after morphia, opium, or hasheesh.

The first act passed off very well, but during the third act, just when I was relating to the Duchesse de Septmonts (played by Croizette) all the ills that had befallen me, Mrs. Clarkson, in my life, just as

I should have commenced my interminable story, I could not remember anything at all. Croizette whispered my first words, but I could only see her lips moving without hearing a word. I then said quite calmly : " The reason I sent for you here, Madame, is because I wanted to apprise you of my reasons for acting as I have done. . . . I have thought it over, and have decided not to tell you them to-day."

Sophie Croizette stared at me terrified, rose and left the stage, her lips trembling and her eyes fixed on me. " What is the matter ? " they said to her, when she sank almost breathless into a chair.

" Sarah has gone mad ! I assure you she has gone quite mad ! She has cut out the whole of her scene with me.—How !—She has cut out two hundred lines ! Why ? I do not know. She seemed quite calm."

All this conversation, which was subsequently retailed to me, took less time that it takes to write it down. Coquelin was warned and he went on the stage to finish the act. After the curtain had fallen, I remained dazed and gloomy at what I had been told. I had been aware of nothing. Under the influence of opium, I had lost my memory for a moment. Happily I recovered it for the few things I had to do in the fifth act, in which I acquitted myself perfectly. I hardly dare confess

that the audience did not notice the accidental cut
that I made in the play of Dumas *fils*.   All's well
that ends well.   But such a lapse might have ter-
minated tragically.

The most extraordinary memory that I have
ever come across was that of Gambetta, the great
tribune.   One evening when I was dining in his
company at the house of Emile de Girardin (it
was I believe in 1869), he asked me to recite some
verses of Victor Hugo, of whom he confessed himself the most fervent admirer.   I acceded with
good grace to his request.

" Shall we repeat *Hernani* together ? " he in-
quired.

" But I do not remember the part of Dona
Sol," I answered ; " I learnt it at the Conservatoire, but . . ."

He burst out laughing.

" What ?   You have no recollection of those
splendid verses that you learned four years ago !
Well, I learned the whole piece, yes, the whole
piece, and I'll say it to you."

And he recited all the first act without omitting
or spoiling a single verse, to the great delight and
surprise of the audience consisting of five persons,
among whom were Edmond About, the famous
author of *Le Roman d'un brave homme*, and Albert
Wolf, critic on the staff of the *Figaro*.   Amused by

our admiring astonishment, Gambetta offered to repeat *Ruth et Booz*, commencing with the last word of the last verse ; and he recited the whole poem backwards, not verse by verse, but word by word, and he declared that he knew all Hugo and all Ossian in the same way.

Physical Proportions

PHYSICAL qualities, which in all other arts or professions may be regarded as secondary, accessory, or negligible, are all-important to the actor, and this is not the least of the difficulties of the career.

It is a matter of indifference whether a painter, a musician, or a sculptor be tall or short. He may be as big as Goliath or as little as David. He may be afflicted with all the infirmities of nature, may lean on crutches or limp, without the value of his work being in the least affected.

Beethoven and Berlioz, Michelangelo and Raphael might have been club-footed ; nobody would have remembered it. The dramatic artist, on the other hand, is considerably handicapped in this respect. An actor must be tall, have a good figure, an expressive and pleasing face, and nothing that detracts from the general harmony of his body. If he be under the average height, he is precluded from appearing on the stage, unless he possess an extraordinary genius which

42

would make the most exacting spectator forget the defect which nothing could overcome. Here study and the most resolute determination are powerless, and it can well happen that a man with remarkable aptitude for the stage, who, had he been a few inches taller, would have left a glorious name, is obliged to abandon the art that is dearest to him.

From the actress the spectator demands even more. So far as she is concerned, the most perfect technique cannot compensate for the physical grace, the charm, and the fascination that emanates from woman. No doubt by will power and by work she may prolong her youth, and even after middle age give the illusion of freshness and adolescence. But if she lacks the necessary figure, if she is without the minimum of gracefulness, or is defective in originality, if nature has endowed her so unkindly that she cannot appear on the stage without repelling the audience at first sight, she will do wise to abandon all her hopes of succeeding as an actress.

The advice that I have to give artists at this stage is to take stock of their capabilities, and to refrain from embarking upon a dramatic career, unless they are fitted by nature for exposure to the public gaze ; to renounce the theatre, if they are not made for the theatre. Just as it would

be foolish to attempt to act on the stage if a
person has a poor memory, if the words and replies
imperfectly learned and assimilated escape recollection, so it would be vain, illusory, and absurd
to fly in the face of what I would call the " dic-
tates of nature," and to ignore a few elementary
rules. Here more than elsewhere the maxim :
" Know thyself ! " is appropriate. The aspiring
artist who tries to blind himself to his physical
defects, who attempts to efface the most prominent
of these by his other merits, runs the grave risk
of foundering in the most disastrous of ship-
wrecks.

But I have not said all I have to say about this
question. It is not enough to withdraw from
the theatre if, despite undoubted gifts, an aspirant
is too badly served in respect of figure, face, and
form to be able to appear on the stage with
advantage ; it also behoves the aspirant who pos-
sesses the minimum of the requisite qualities to
adapt himself to the rôle that best suits him.

There is a fitness of things intellectual, and a
fitness of things physical, and the latter should
receive as much attention as the former. Every
actor is not made to don the costume of Romeo
and every actress will not succeed in the rôle of
Chimène. It happens too often at the theatre
that artists, who, after all, are subject to a man-

ager's authority, impersonate incongruous characters very much to their detriment.   Certainly
the part that technique can play is great, but I
repeat it is not all—and he who compromises
his career by playing the part of a greybeard
with a youthful voice, or that of a bashful lover
with a heavy and tottering gait will overtax his
strength, the while he forgets the most elementary
counsels of wisdom.   If it be an excellent prin-
ciple of government to allot each man to his post
and adapt his employment to his capabilities, it
is an even more admirable rule for the theatre.
But accurate discernment, especially when turned
by an individual on himself, is one of the rarest
qualities in the world.   The actor is too prone
to exaggerate his powers ; he wants to play
Hamlet when his appearance is more suitable to
King Lear.   An actress may imagine that she
makes an enchanting *soubrette*, when her age has
already placed her in the category of duennas.
Renounce the stage if you are unfit by nature,
or accept only those parts which you are able
to play, and which your physical characteristics
and your appearance do not enjoin you to refuse.
Perfect beauty is not essential to the theatre ;
an actress may have an ordinary face and yet be
perfectly charming on the stage, provided she is
well proportioned, that is to say, if she has a

small face, a long neck, a short figure, and long legs and arms.   It is rare for a woman's face to be entirely ugly, especially if she is animated by the desire to please ; and this should always be the aim of an actress, whatever her part, even if it be that of a mother-in-law.   It is all-important for the artist who is destined for the stage to be well proportioned :   the expression of the face changes according to the feelings to be expressed. A man can succeed in the theatre if he is ugly :   if he is tall and well built, he will be able to play lovers' parts.   His face lends itself to modification much more easily than that of a woman, thanks to the device of beards, moustaches, and wigs.

An actor of great talent and rare elegance, a great favourite with Russian ladies because of his handsome appearance and splendid proportions, refused to shave his moustache.   One day the Emperor Alexander II said to him :

" I see, Berton, that *Adrienne Lecouvreur* is to be played to-morrow.   You are surely not going to play Maurice of Saxony with your moustache ? "

It was a command, polite but imperative, and Berton shaved his moustache.   It was a disaster. The Russian ladies felt that they were insulted. It is said that one of them fainted, and the Emperor, on inquiring the cause of her indisposition,

learned that the shorn lip of the actor was responsible for the young lady's illness. Alexander
repaired to the stage, and seeing Maurice of
Saxony, approached him.

" You are very ugly without your moustache,
my good fellow."

And turning to the manager who was bowing
low :

" Withdraw the play until the poor fellow
recovers his hair."

Berton had a very short lip, so thin and indrawn
that the upper part of his mouth could not be
distinguished. This man who had magnificent
eyes and a manly and distinguished face, also
had a hare lip, which without his moustache gave
him an appearance which provoked laughter.

It is impossible for a woman to gain admit-
tance to a dramatic school or to enter any theatre,
even as a dancer, with such a painful defect.
Actresses, like actors, can alter and almost transform their faces by means of a wig. But I would
repeat that the fact of being endowed with the
proportions requisite to lend beauty to the whole
appearance relieves a man or woman from worry-
ing about the faces. The harmony of which I
speak is impossible if one is either too tall or too
short. Extremely tall women in the theatre,
even if they are well proportioned, are out of

place.   They always spoil the perspective, even
when they enter from the end of a park or a
gallery.   French actors are usually of an average
height ; they have a horror of acting with extremely tall women.   For a man extreme tallness
is not troublesome ; it is suitable to tragedy or
to leading parts.   On the other hand, little women
are able to play simple maidens or young pages.
An actor who is too short has no future.

One of my godfathers (I had three), a pretentious and self-opinionated man, with a slow and
slovenly way of speaking, once told me :

" You know, my child, that you are not plump
enough to realize your ambition.   I have seen
Mlle. Georges, and when she was on the stage,
one saw only her ; everybody else disappeared."

" But, godfather, this would upset the equili-
brium of tragedies."

" That is a silly thing to say, child ; I tell
you that she put everybody in her pocket."

" Well, for my part, I cannot imagine Pyrrhus
in the pocket of Hermione, nor Hippolyte in
that of Phèdre."

And the old rascal muttered under his breath :

" Don't worry, child, it is you they will put in
their pockets."

Now, although Mlle. Georges was a fine figure
of a woman, she lacked talent, as I was told by

Legouve and M. Thiers, two men whose judgment I greatly esteemed.

May the shade of my godfather pardon me : my extreme slenderness (which people went so far as to accuse me of cultivating expressly for purposes of advertisement) was compensated by the proportions of my body, and it has not been easy for people to put me in their pockets.

To summarize, the jury of the Conservatoire, entrusted with the admission of potential dramatic artists, ought to take special note of the bodily proportions of aspirants, and refuse to admit little women with big heads or lads with long bodies, supported by short and bandy legs—even as comic actors. It is better for the laughter they provoke to be the result of their studies rather than that of their physical imperfections. For I refuse the title of artist to those who owe their reputations to a physical deformity. I regard them as buffoons.

The Voice

THE voice is the dramatic artist's most necessary instrument. It is the voice that fixes the attention of the public, and effects contact between the artist and the audience. It must have all the harmonies, grave, plaintive, vibrant, and metallic. A defective voice will always preclude an artist from achieving the complete development of his art, however intelligent he may be. He will be up against an intangible, but yet very real, obstacle. The shrewdness of the actor may for a moment evade the difficulty, but his career will be confined to a special line of business. And specialization in a line of business is a drawback, and a sign of an imperfection of artistic powers. He who specializes and never plays any parts but those of a valet or of the *jeune premier* is not a complete artist. But it often happens that a manager or the public will confine the unfortunate man to a line of business where he excels and prohibit him from broadening his nature. This is a mistake that cannot be too much regretted.

I never saw Rachel who, it appears, had a full and deep voice, but devoid of light tones, which fact prevented her from playing comedy, in spite of several pleasing attempts. Yet it is unbelievable that this illustrious tragedienne, who died too young, could never have overcome the difficulties of a voice that was a trifle sombre, although full of charm and of an extraordinary fulness.

With actors and actresses the voice alters almost every three or four years, and often changes its timbre. This fact enables certain artists who have been out of favour to appear in a good part, to the great astonishment of their friends.

A fine voice is often a baneful gift if the artist uses it only to produce sound. There are young tragediennes who are for ever confined to tragic parts because they have a " fine voice," and this is a lamentable admission when one knows how limited is the career of a tragedienne who only plays tragedy. At the Théâtre Français there is a young artist whom they bury softly under the fine notes of her voice. I have tried to induce her to revolt against this state of affairs, and pointed out to her two or three parts in which she could shine. But she is sweet, and doubtless expends all her energy in *Horace*. And it is a great pity.

Coquelin's was a voice both magnificent and complete. It ranged over all the scales, and had every shade of resonance. If Coquelin had had an ordinary nose, he would certainly have succeeded in some tragic parts.

During a tour we made together in America, he confided to me one day his disappointment.

" Tell me," he remarked, " why I have not succeeded in dramatic parts."

" But, Coquelin," I answered, " it is because of your nose ; it gives you a comical physiognomy in greatness and in sorrow."

" How stupid !   Listen, I will recite *Néron* to you."

I listened to him. To be sure it sounded very well, and his conception of Nero was interesting ; but it would not have done to look at him. The wrinkled forehead, knit brows, fine and piercing glance were not enough to mitigate the comicality of that nose open to all winds, sniffing up the joy of living, and contradicting by its aspect the dramatic expression of the forehead and the eyes. Coquelin was a great actor, but not a great artist. He lacked the notion of harmony, the general idea necessary for the instinctive conception of a character. This is why he could not impersonate Napoleon, in spite of irritation at his failure, and when one day he told me that he proposed to play *Pétrone*, I used all my power to dissuade him from doing so. Nobody equalled nor will equal him for a long time, I fear, in the parts of Molière's valets, where his creations were unique.

For the voice to be really complete it must be very slightly nasal. An artist with a dry voice will never move the public.

Mounet Sully had an admirable voice, capable of every modulation. It is to his strong, vibrant, and melodious voice that he owes the greater part of his reputation. Add to this marvellous voice a finely-proportioned body and a face of flawless beauty, and an artist cannot help winning great popularity.

There are some broken voices that retain a great charm. There are others that grate on the ear. Such voices as these are not broken, but shattered. A certain tragedienne possessing such a voice, who is beloved in spite of this defect by the public of the Comédie Française, plays a type of realism which the ignorant mistake for talent. Since here, I will also mention the extremely melodious and metallic voice of Julia Bartet. This voice has enabled her to attack with equal success tragedy, comedy, and the drama, thereby pursuing a complete career. She will remain one of the stars of Molière's House.

The finest voice I have ever heard throughout

my endless career is that of Solidini, the great
Italian actor.   It was a whole orchestra ; all the
notes issued from that throat in perfect unison
with the text.   Fury, sorrow, placidity were suc-
ceed^d by glacial irony, and all these manifestations were so modulated that it was impossible
to perceive the bridge that connected them all
together.   Moreover, Solidini was a magnificent
artist.

Another marvellous voice is that of Lucien
Guitry.   He has played great tragic and dramatic
parts with a success equal to that of his manifold
interpretations of modern plays.   The latter, I
grant, do not require any special voice ; but the
artist was not able to reject the gift that nature
had offered him, and his prodigious talent
is doubled by the indefinable charm of his
voice.

It is a fault at the Conservatoire to overwork
the voice in the case of young people, especially
when they are destined for tragedy.   How many
children of fifteen or eighteen have I seen, whose
careers have been irreparably damaged by an
unskilful or indifferent teacher ?

It was my good fortune to have three teachers,
famous artists of great authority and great humanity : MM. Provost, Samson, and Régnier.
These men loved their pupils and guided them

wisely. Their chief concern was not their own, but their pupils' success.

I remember that Provost vigorously refused to allow me to compete in the examination three months after my admission, as he considered that I was too young and too delicate. He also opposed granting me the first prize on my examination.

"If you give her the first prize, which I grant she deserves, she will leave the Conservatoire too soon. She needs another year of study without tiring the voice."

This was related to me by Régnier one day when, being in a bad temper, I was complaining of Provost. He was not to have the pleasure of finishing the tuition of his little rebel, as he called me, and it was Samson who prepared me for my second examination. Thanks to these remarkable teachers, my voice remained unspoilt, and yet I was a devotee of Tragedy.

The voices of young people must be spared as much as possible. There is always a great inclination to cultivate loudness when a pupil has a fine voice. Artists, even the greatest of them, frequently speak too loudly, and as an example I will mention Lucien Guitry, who knows how to give quite a perfect impression of violent energy, and will then fall back on a single metallic word to close his period.   He knows so well how to choose the most resounding word.   The choice of words in a sentence requires a special study to itself.

A modern artist who had a charming voice was Suzanne Reichemberg.   Her voice was soft and limpid, like a pretty stream tumbling over rocks ; but this delightful actress had one fault : that of clinging to juvenile parts.   When she wanted to change her line of business, her voice would not adapt itself, because it had only been exercised in one direction.   Reichemberg was obliged to give up the stage, although several years of theatrical life yet remained to her.

The very great actress Réjane, the rival of Duse, another great artist to whom she was much superior, had a taking voice.   This voice had several broken notes, which precluded the wonder-ful interpreter from playing certain parts that she was anxious to attempt.   Her sense of the fitness of things saved her from this temptation.   She felt that, owing to her voice, these parts of a purely lyrical character were beyond her.   But how much grander was the result she obtained in certain others, where she realized the ideal by her conception of realism.

When listening to it I have very often regretted not being the creator or deft fashioner to impart to that warm and pleasing voice the trifling thing that was lacking, not in order to be the voice of a complete artist, which Réjane was, but to enable the latter to satisfy her love of the ideal.

I have mentioned Duse. I would not have it thought that I deny talent to this great artist, but I much prefer Réjane, whom she resembled without having the latter's Parisian polish.

Actors and actresses have very often held the attention of the public merely by the tone of their voices. This is not enough. The voice is an instrument which the artist must learn to use with suppleness and sureness, as if it were a limb.

Some there are who are the slaves of their voices : they are seduced by the sound of words, and are carried away by the cadence of verses or phrases. They have become enamoured of the vocal effects, and this is a most pernicious habit.

I remember, when I was a young girl and followed with great enthusiasm the performances at the Comédie Française, the effect obtained by a tragedienne, skilful in tricks but lacking talent, when in *Andromaque* she cried frantically to Oreste :

" Why assassinate him ; what has he done ; by what right ? "

She yelled these three phrases, then relapsed, and added calmly in a hollow voice :

" Who told you ? "

Prompted by the claque, the public burst into great applause.

I devoted eight days to an attempt to imitate this guttural " Who told you ? " and as I despaired of being able to do so, I confided my disappointment to M. Provost.   This charming man asked me :

" Look, if you had the strength to play such a part, how would you say this verse yourself ? "

Thrown back on my instincts, I declaimed the verse in my own way.

" Well, then, my child, keep this for yourself later on, and forget the ' Who told you ' of that fine voice."

This fashion of producing vocal effects is happily lost.   Here and there in the provinces a tragedian or tragedienne has preserved this bad tradition.   They can only be successful with that special public which goes to see a tragedy in order to watch at the same passage for the same effect produced by the same means, the echo of which has come down to it through successive generations.

To know how to use the voice, it is needful to have a musical ear (this is not an injunction to practise music !).   This musical ear co-ordinates the natural sounds which the vocal chords emit ; it guides them, subjects them to a rule, and preserves them pure and healthy. It enables the speaker immediately to adapt himself to altered acoustics consequent upon changing his theatre or upon variations in the size of the audience.

There are artists who enrapture the author of a new play during rehearsals, but stagger him on the first night. The artist in question may be quite intelligent and say his lines correctly, but he lacks vocal powers. He enunciates his part with the requisite energy, but the words do not travel beyond the first rows of the orchestra. And as the author and the director and manager are in a little structure which protects them from the cold two yards away from the actor, all the words are absorbed in the little refuge of the areopagus sitting in judgment. On the day of the first performance the structure is removed and the artist is not heard. His performance may be remarkable, but only ten or twenty people hear it. The chief scene is a failure, and the author tears his hair. Consequently it behoves actors to pay attention to delivery. This, too, should be taught by the Conservatoire. It is a piece of extremely hard work that must be tackled. To the person who perseveres the reward is not delayed.

" What great progress you have made since last year," you are told by a sympathetic relative.

And one reads in a criticism :

" Mlle. X, whom we used to reproach with feeble intonation, seems to us to have progressed. We did not miss a word, etc., etc."

It might be supposed that delivery depends upon pronunciation, but this is an error. There are artists who pronounce admirably, but do not know how to make their voices carry, just as there are others who scream and murder their words, which mingle with the vibrations of the words shouted immediately before.

Delivery depends upon the extent to which the mouth is opened, and particularly upon the manner of breathing. Never get out of breath. Sufficient air must be inhaled for four lines or twenty-six words at least. This is an excellent breathing exercise. Four lines cannot be said with one inspiration at the first attempt, but this can be managed quickly enough by letting the air escape slowly and gently with the words.

There was a famous professor, a shareholder in the Comédie Française, M. Talbot by name, who was my first tutor and gave me excellent advice, but towards the end of his career he became a trifle eccentric. He would make his pupils lie flat ; then he would place the marble slab of his mantelpiece on their stomachs, and say :

" Now breathe . . . and say your part."

The worthy Talbot perhaps exaggerated the proceedings a little, but his first method of respiration was excellent. The finest voice is not proof against shortness of breath. To master this instrument, it is essential to achieve perfection in breathing.

In Phèdre I succeeded in saying the following four lines in one breath, and giving the words their necessary modulation :

> Hélas ! ils se voyaient avec pleine licence.
> Le ciel, de leurs soupirs approuvait l'innocence.
> Ils suivaient sans remords leur penchant amoureux
> Tous les jours se levaient clairs et sereins pour eux !

These sad and harmonious lines, recited in a melodious chant, were applauded by the public which felt their charm without knowing its cause.

Francisque Sarcey, the great critic, and Jules Lemaître, the fastidious writer, were most enthusiastic over the method of saying these four lines in one clear stream of sound, as Jules Lemaître described it.

Pronunciation

PRONUNCIATION is one of the primordial qualities of the art of speaking.
Although the will is the surest factor in
all the acts of life, physical defects have also to be
reckoned with. A jaw that is a trifle large gives
impetus to words ; a high roof to the mouth
favours sonority ; closely set teeth prevent hissing, while teeth set widely apart promote it.

It is therefore incumbent on the artist to
employ all possible means to remedy these little
defects, some of which can certainly be mitigated.
For instance, I was acquainted with an artist,
accustomed to play great dramatic parts, whose
widely spaced teeth gave her diction a strident
hiss that was excruciating. I advised her when
" making up " to put a little pink wax inside her
upper jawbone ; the device succeeded perfectly,
and when I met her again, after having lost sight
of her for many months, she told me that she
had continued to use this little device, and could
not do without it even at home.

Small and shapely jaws are certainly prettier than large jaws, but in the case of dramatic artists they are not so favourable for delivery, and for this there is no remedy. The only compensation for the possession of a small jaw is that the face gains in prettiness.

The same consideration applies to the roof of the mouth. It cannot be altered in any way. The actor who enunciates clearly will always make himself heard, and for that very reason understood.

An actor who lacks a fine voice may remedy the defect by perfect articulation, and create a public for himself. Saint-Germain was for twenty years the favourite of a public which frequented the Vaudeville and the Gymnase. He had completely lost his voice, and spoke like a person afflicted with laryngitis, but he had realized that articulation was an indispensable asset to the actor as well as to the advocate, and the public agreed with him.

Of course, it is not necessary to articulate all the syllables of a word to the same extent as the Southerners do, but it is essential that the ear should detect the suppressed syllable. A native of Touraine says *manqment*, a native of Bordeaux says *manquement*, the Parisian artist strikes th happy medium by proper accentuation of syllables.

In order to be sure of his articulation, an artist must learn his parts by muttering them to himself, and he must have perfect control over his jaw.   Incoherency is often only a sign of loss of memory.   It must also be added that mediocre artists are satisfied if they get near enough to the precise word, but this little book is not designed for them.

However, I should not like sincere artists with moderate gifts to think that I confound them with the mediocre.   There are modest artists who often deserve the gratitude of authors for the atmosphere which they create in spite of their humble rôles.   They love our art passionately, although they have not in their hands all the trump-cards necessary to crown their careers with triumph.   They belong to the great family, of which the others are only parasites.

The real difficulty of articulation in the theatre as well as at the bar is to know what value to give to words.   Only intelligence can guide the actor here, and there is no method for transforming a stupid being into an intelligent being.

I advise young actors to see and hear Lucien Guitry as often as possible.   They should study the talent of this great comedian, and they will find that when he seems to hesitate he is about to utter a sentence which is the touchstone of a whole psychical state, and in this phrase the tonic accent will be on the word that is bound to enlighten the hearer. Lucien Guitry is the greatest actor of our age, none has played nor will play, as he did, the part of Flambeau in *l'Aiglon.* I, whose great joy it was to have him for partner, used to listen to him passionately ; his art is incomparable. He never repeats himself, and yet is always the same personage creating the same atmosphere necessary to the play. He is the finest model that can be recommended to the younger generation.

The most lamented and exquisite Réjane was also an artist in whom could be discerned the sentiment of truth, a sincere emotion, a great revelation of thought in all the joyous and sorrowful parts which she interpreted. Like Guitry, Réjane had the gift of laughter and of tears with the same measure of poignant emotion and contagious gaiety.

I made enemies of Irving and Coquelin because I said in private conversation that Coquelin was a remarkable actor but not an artist, while Irving was a mediocre actor, but a great artist. I do not retract. Irving was defective in articulation and pronunciation, but his expression was profoundly thoughtful. He had a love of the beautiful ; his costumes always exhibited great historical truth ; he read up his subjects most scrupulously, and the staging of his plays was marked by a breadth of study, a taste, and an accuracy such as attracted the public in crowds to the performances at the Lyceum, of which Irving was manager.   Thanks to him, the English theatre gained a great reputation throughout the world, and the grateful English laid his bones in Westminster Abbey, the last refuge of great men who have rendered service to their country.

Irving was for the English theatre what Antoine was for the French theatre, the finger-post of a new phase.   Yet these finger-posts did not point in the same direction.   The Englishman guided his public to the Past with a wealth of research and idealism, while the other halted on the threshold of realism and compelled his public to penetrate into the labyrinth of human passions. Both were great apostles of our art, and yet neither the one nor the other was a great actor. But what artists !

I cannot say as much of Constant Coquelin, who was really a very great actor, less finished than Lucien Guitry, but quite as wonderful in the perfection of his articulation; his admirable voice lent perfect modulation to every phrase, his laugh was unique, and the most doleful minds, the most poignant griefs yielded to his riotous humour.

He was above all a great comic actor, irradiating
Molière's plays with a fiery and vivifying sun ;
he did not perhaps always perceive their profound
irony, but his performance remained superb.

The younger generation of his age produced
many imitators. But none of them has that gay
and charming voice, that volubility of words
dashing against each other without a single jarring
note, that thorough mastery of respiration. The
imitators of this great actor are well enough in
their way, but that is all.

I have wandered from my subject, to which I
must return. Young actors must be able to
articulate ; whatever talent they may have, they
will never achieve real success unless the public
can grasp the meaning of what it hears, and a
lost word often breaks up a whole sentence.

Articulation must not be confused with pronunciation ; these two servants of thought are
twin sisters, it is true, but they are different in
several respects. Defects of pronunciation are
frequently shown in an accent due to the actor's
place of birth. Some emphasize the *t*, or the *p*,
others roll the *r* or burr it ; there are artists
who clip the *a* or drone the *o* ; these are
peculiarities easy to correct. It is enough to
make up one's mind to do it. But many artists
do not give themselves the trouble to remove

these little defects, to which the public appear to pay no heed.

During my time at the Théâtre Français there was a talented actor who said in Emile Augier's *Philiberte* : " Il faudrait la potrie en donger pour que notre grond coeur daigne se deronger."

A few of the spectators nudged each other, but the others did not detect anything amiss. And this actor, I repeat, had a delightful talent. The public forgives actors their little defects of pronunciation, provided they articulate the words they have to say so as to make them understood.

There are actors who bleat, and this is a defect due not to pronunciation, but to the voice. Either the nose is blocked at the base, or the vocal chords are congested.

I knew an actor possessed of superb talent whose bleating made one shudder. The public had accepted him, and he was even a favourite. I played with him in two plays where he was above all criticism. And when I went on tour with him to play the two plays in question, the foreign public could not get used to this bleating, and this actor had to return to France.

One trick of pronunciation consists in deliberately clipping a word in order to accentuate it. This is not a question of a personal and involuntary peculiarity. Again, the method of pronunciation is not the same for verse as it is for prose. Actors who recite verse are obliged continuously to pronounce the mute *e* in order to leave the feet and the value of the verse intact, while in prose the *es* are skipped with the grace necessary to the easing of sentences. For example :

> Comme il fait noir dans la vallé*e*
> J'ai cru qu'un*e* forme voilé*e*
> Flottait là-bas sur la prairi*e*
> Son pied rasait l'herb*e* fleuri*e*
> C'est une étrange rêveri*e* . . .
> etc., etc., etc.

If this couplet were turned into prose, it would be said much more quickly without taking account of the mute *es*. *Qu'uneformvoilée* would be said almost in one word.

These differences of pronunciation due to the accentuation or the elision of the mute *e* bring me to that peculiarity of the Southern accent which emphasizes all the vowels. There are cases where this method of speaking, although quite French, becomes ridiculous and destroys all the illusion upon which the theatre lives ; you have only to listen to a Marseilles artist interpreting the part of a Swedish pastor.

Mounet Sully and his brother Paul Mounet, both born at Bergerac, had a very pronounced accent of the soil when they came to Paris. Mounet Sully laboured with tenacity to render his delivery elegant, and he quickly succeeded in doing so, preserving of his Southern accent only his rather broad *rs* ; but his brother, who was engaged in medical and surgical studies, considered it useless to embark on this additional labour. When he had passed his examination and was smitten by the craze of the theatre, the support and encouragement of Mounet enabled him to realize his dream. It was too late to lose any time, and he decided to foist his Southern accent upon the Parisian public, who accepted it with good grace. For myself I found that this circumstance considerably spoiled the actor's talent, and imparted to Don Diègue, to old Horace, and especially to King Œdipus a doleful vulgarity for the spectator who realized the incomparable greatness of Mounet in the latter part.

We have among our great actors a few foreign comedians whose accent might be expected to make a more painful impression on us than the rustic accent of our provincials. Nevertheless, I find that De Max, who has never lost his Roumanian accent and interprets the greatest figures of the French theatre, is never vulgar and does not shock the public ear. He often lets himself be carried beyond the limits of accuracy by his comprehension, which is always ideal, of the characters he impersonates ; he is sometimes extravagant, but he is never vulgar.

An accent that it is really impossible to suppress entirely is the Auvergne accent. When I passed my first examination at the Conservatoire, I was petrified on hearing a young man announce to the jury in a thunderous voice :

" Mademoiselle Chara Bernhardt ! "

This man was a prizeman of the preceding year, and in spite of his first prize for tragedy, no manager would engage him ; he was obliged to become a prompter, and I met him again at the Comédie Française where he was second prompter. One evening during the performance of *Gabrielle*, a stupid play by Emile Augier, the actor Thirion, who had lost his memory in the vineyards of the Lord, came to a stop. My prompter, Leautaud, gave him his line like this :

" Cha, Madame, chest une injuchtiche ! "

(Ça, Madame, c'est une injustice.)

And Thirion repeated word for word with the Auvergne accent the reply sent him by the worthy prompter. Madeleine Brohan and I who were on the stage could not repress our hilarity, and the public, very amused and good-humoured, shrieked with laughter. But the scandal assumed

an unpleasant shape for the poor actor. The
Superintendent of Theatres fined Thirion a thousand francs, but Leautaud retained his post.

The Gascon accent is less brutal and less heavy
than the Dordogne accent, and brisker than the
Bordeaux accent, which slurs. Actors who are
born or brought up in Bordeaux find it difficult
to get rid of their accent. When Cora Lapar-
cerie recited verse, an art in which she excelled,
this defect almost entirely disappeared, but in the
modern plays in which she is fond of appearing,
the accent often emerges most inconveniently
for the public ear. But this is nothing to the
suburban accent.

For my part I derive no pleasure from hearing
an actor, even a talented one, who pronounces
mé, té, cé, instead of mes, tes, ces, or who ejacu-
lates with a genteel movement of the fan :

" Oui, c'é tu homme charmant ! "

And this particular accent the Conservatoire
does not attempt to remove.

When I was appointed a teacher at the Conservatoire, I, of course, believed that my judgment would be deferred to in the case of pupils
confided to my care. I soon perceived my mistake. Among the young girls whom I had to
instruct in the dramatic art was a pretty suburban
girl who possessed a revolting accent.

" Oh, Médème," she said to me one day, " mon auteur préféré, cé Voltère ! "

With great patience I applied myself to the task of teaching her the way to say a Suzanne scene from the *Mariage de Figaro.* After five lessons that I deemed to have been useless, I told the child that she would do better to resume her old profession of dressmaker ; she went away and complained. She was pretty and not at all shy, and her appeal was successful. I sent in my resignation.

I met this little person again in a provincial theatre, where I had gone to give a performance of *La Dame aux Camélias.* She came to me smiling, still attractive and suburban, and when I questioned her about her career, she said :

" Oh, it's all right, Médème, I gain my living."

She played servants' parts and juvenile parts. She seemed happy, but I felt sorry for her ; I knew she was condemned to earn her two or three hundred francs a month as long as she was young. For she was small and slender and could not change her line of business. What would she do afterwards ? She would become a dresser or a theatre attendant. So many artists finish in this way.

I know a young actress of talent, of great talent, who plays not only in modern plays, but also appears in classic rôles. She has a suburban accent that is most painful to hear, and it is a pity, for she will certainly have to exert considerable efforts to reach the first place that she covets. There is no need to mention her name. If she wishes to correct herself, she will perhaps be enlightened on reading these lines. Her art, which is personal and sincere, will gain in elegance.

Many actors and actresses have an accent peculiar to themselves, which renders imitation easy.

She who writes these lines clenches the teeth a little too much, especially at dress rehearsals or on the first night when she has an attack of stage fright. Moreover, thanks to this defect and to an exaggerated slenderness, caricaturists and imitators (who in reality resemble each other) are able to gratify themselves to their hearts' content. And many owe their little fame only to a taste that is more or less dubious. No doubt it was the will of fate that these caricatures and imitations, far from injuring the artist in question, have rendered her popular, and the public have pardoned her this fault which weighs so little by the side of her poetic gifts and the sincerity of her art.

I have already referred to the splendid quality of the voices of Julia Bartet and of Suzanne Reichemberg. Their pronunciation is no less faultless ; often when my advice is asked, I send pupils to them, in order that they may profit from listening to the elegant delivery of these artists who have no singularity of articulation and no accent.

It is not enough to overcome all personal imperfections of pronunciation. Pronunciation must be learnt in order to impart to words and phrases their proper value. Many defects remain to be overcome. Laxity in this respect brings the prosody of an author into disfavour ; over-elaboration tires the public, while slovenliness irritates it. It is therefore necessary to keep one's ears open, to curb words or to accentuate them.

When an actor like Guitry studies a part, he has no need to make a laborious effort ; he passes into the proper atmosphere directly. Whether the sentiments be tragical, ironical, or comical, he adopts them as his own forthwith. He has nothing to seek, no effort to make, nothing to suppress or to emphasize, because he begins immediately to live the life of the character he impersonates. A modern part should never be overworked. It is enough to enter into the various feelings of the character in question, and then to plunge into action ; the genuine accent which you are moved to utter in the first lines will soon be reflected on the public.

I have heard it said by contemporaries of Talma
that this artist never felt emotion, and counselled
his young pupils above all to control the passions
they would have to feign.

Moreover, this assertion was endorsed by
Coquelin with some asperity, and I am convinced
it was owing to this method that he was never
able to excite the enthusiasm of his audience in
the pathetic scenes of which he was so enamoured.

His success in exciting laughter was extraordinary, but he always failed in tragedy, and
an ironical friend said to him one day in front of
me when he was complaining of his want of
success in Jean d'Acier :

" Look here, my friend, you are admirable in
simulating passion and emotion, but your nose
does you an injustice, it is too comical for words."

Constant Coquelin was thoughtful for a moment, and then turning to me asked :

" Is that your opinion ? "

I was amazed that he could take such an argument seriously ; I answered evasively by citing
the case of Lekain, a tragedian of great reputation
who owned the same excessively *retroussé* nose,
and whose other features resembled those of
Coquelin.

But henceforth this great comic actor had
recourse to nose paste for all the great parts that

he had to perform, and his nose and chin underwent successive transformations. Yet the public remained cold before the sentiments of despair that he, faithful to his method, expressed without feeling.

I have seen this artist sleeping soundly on the stage sheltered by supers during two or three minutes when he had nothing to say. A young actor named Chabert, who was very attached to him, would wake him up, and Coquelin, refreshed by three minutes of absolute isolation, would resume his part with zest. I was amazed at this.

Yes, I am opposed to this method, as I contend it is necessary to feel all the sentiments that agitate the soul of the character it is desired to represent. The artist's personality must be left in his dressing-room ; his soul must be denuded of its own sensations and clothed with the base or noble qualities he is called upon to exhibit.

I once had an Italian chambermaid who, returning one evening from seeing me in *Phèdre*, said :

" Oh ! Madame was so lovely that I didn't recognize Madame ! "

And no compliment ever went more direct to my heart. One must love, weep, suffer, and even die. Ah ! I see the smiles and hear the comments : yet you who have died thousands of different deaths are still alive and have reached an advanced age.

Well, yes, it is true, I am still living, but I have touched real death in my different deaths. Sometimes it had taken more than an hour for me to come to life. My face has been bloodless, my heart has almost stopped beating, my lungs have stopped breathing ; but I have retained the will power necessary to resume my true personality, just as it is necessary to retain sufficient presence of mind to remember one's part on the stage.

The secret of our art consists in preventing the audience from recognizing it to be illusion : not for a moment must the audience think that what is represented has not happened ; we must keep the audience in the environment whither the author intended to transport it, creating the atmosphere by our sincerity, and the audience, breathless and distraught, must not be allowed to recapture its freewill until the fall of the curtain.

What has been called the labour of our art can only be the quest of truth. Plays in verse no doubt require interpreters possessing special gifts. But it is always the artist who is closest to the real in the ideal who will triumph.

Gesture

GESTURE does not mean the movements of the limbs solely, but the attitude of the body as a whole. With the actor everything must be simultaneously alive, and give expression to the deep feelings that animate him— eye, hand, position of the chest, inflexion of the head all contributing to the total effect. Now an actor who is tall, of agreeable figure, with a fine and elegant voice, a good disposition, and a keen intelligence will achieve but indifferent success if he be unable to give outward semblance to successive psychic states. The external side of art is sometimes the whole of art ; at least it is that which strikes the eye. If the actor who knows his part perfectly, who has fully assumed the personality of his hero remains motionless, with his arms tight against his body, his head always inclined in the same direction, his eye dead or dull, if the public does not feel that it is confronted by a being of flesh and blood, no effect will be produced. And in this respect the reverse of what is generally asserted holds good. In order to convince others, the actor must be convinced himself ; but it is not sufficient that he himself feels the violent crises of passion ; he must give outward expression to them.

But gesture must not be a disorderly business. Just as delivery does not comprise only savage shouts, and just as the public will tire of a boisterous beginner who does not know how to moderate his voice, so it will not be long in finding ridiculous an actor whose unruly attitudes do not in any way correspond to phases of the mind. Moderation is the rule in all things.   Man is not indefinitely cold, languishing, or indifferent ; serenity of mind does not persist without interruption ; nor can man remain a prey to continuous emotion, expending himself in various passions, and maintaining for ever a flashing eye.

Gesture, like delivery, can be mastered by dint of study and becomes perfect in course of time.   But in no case can study take the place of nature, the innate gifts which constitute the very essence of talent or of genius.   As a general rule, one might say to an artist : " You may over-excite your emotions, and get accustomed to varying your psychic states and translating them into action ; but there is no example on record of an actor who has attained to the front rank in his art without a vocation which was manifested betimes.   A great actor can no more be made artificially than a great musician or a great painter."

SECOND PART

The Moral Qualities necessary to the Actor

The Actor's Rôle

THE rôle of the actor has become increasingly important throughout the transformations of dramatic art. The theatre of antiquity, like modern opera, relied on mass movement ; crowds lent it a sustained movement ; consequently personal qualities only assumed secondary importance. It will be remembered that in the first Greek dramas the individuals were almost drowned in the chorus. But, as by degrees dramatists applied themselves to the analysis of sentiments, the study of the human soul, and the portrayal of passions, love, hate, vengeance, cupidity, etc., the actor's art developed, exacting greater study, and becoming more complex and less easily acquired. The more tragedy or comedy evolved, and tragedy and comedy remained separate until Shakespeare's time (as far as Europe was concerned this lasted until the advent of Romanticism)—the greater was the stress put upon the personal value of the interpreters. The actor's profession became

83

specialized : in antiquity any citizen of Athens or of Corinth might have been called upon to impersonate Prometheus, Xerxes, or Jupiter. Nearer to our own time, Shakespeare and Molière, who performed in their own plays, appear already as glorious exceptions. The actor of our time remains simply an actor, and his task is big enough and toilsome enough to absorb all his energy.

It is true that there has been a recent tendency for crowds to be put on the stage again ; the intention being to depict social evils, and give utterance to collective sentiments—and it might be supposed that in these circumstances the actor would lack an incentive to display his special abilities. One example of these new works is *The Weavers* of Gerhardt Hauptmann ; but the contemporary author—as Ibsen in *The Enemy of the People* or Björnson in *Beyond Our Power*—takes care to leave each man his special features, and the rôle of the actor, instead of being facilitated, is rendered more onerous, for he must express his own emotions and form part of the collective soul at the same time. It is therefore permissible to conclude that as the dramatist's art moves towards perfection, more and more work will be imposed upon the actor who intends to keep pace with its progress.

It might be a matter for surprise that so many

comedians and tragedians of the first rank can be quoted in modern times, while so few persons of exceptional talent can be placed to the credit of past ages. But the simple reason is that these persons of exceptional gifts either did not exist or found no scope for their abilities.

In our day, the intrinsic value of a play assuredly counts for much in the reception it will meet with from the public ;—but the part of the actor is hardly less great than that of the scenario or the mode of treatment.

If first-rate parts are entrusted to bad actors, it is most likely that the comedy, in spite of all its merits, will be hissed off the stage or withdrawn from the theatre. Works that have moved, roused, and astonished successive generations will leave the public cold and even hostile if they do not find proper interpreters. *Le Cid, Polyeucte, Tartuffe, Andromaque*, would only be ridiculous, despite their literary beauties and their powerful portrayals of passions, if the parts were entrusted to incapable actors. But the contrary is not quite accurate : a very bad tragedy or a deplorable drama entrusted to actors of the first class never remains a long time on the bills ; but a mediocre work—instances are numerous—will last to the hundredth performance or longer, if it be assisted by interpreters of ample powers. In this actors resemble those musical virtuosi whose prodigious talents bestow fame upon pieces of music that are scarcely worth hearing. We cannot therefore overestimate the value of those who play in modern drama. And it is not enough for an author to have composed a comedy of high literary merit or of subtle psychology : he must also discover suitable interpreters, and the latter must combine the rare and manifold qualities that make up a great actor. To be quite truthful, it must be confessed that actors of the first water are not more plentiful than playwrights of genius.

Instruction

IF we consider the matter carefully, it will be plain that the actor's most important quality—or better, his primary duty—is comprehensive study. To be sure, it is good for him to possess imagination, even a strong inventive capacity ; his imagination must play freely, and he must not feel hampered in the expansion of his nature. Art excludes of necessity everything that is stiff and rigid. But nothing can take the place of the study of men and of periods. The character of Cæsar, or of Hamlet, or of Augustus cannot be improvised. If the actor is totally ignorant of history, if he cannot fit characters into their environment, if he is incapable of investing them with the sentiments that were common to their epoch, their generation, their class, even their party, he will never be anything but a second-rate actor. Doubtless this was a matter of less importance in the *grand siècle*, when local colour was systematically banished, and the selection of costumes was held to be secondary. The slight regard paid to historic truth is revealed for example in the language attributed to the characters, and Racine's Mussulmen, in *Bajazet*, or the Jews in *Athalie*, or the Greeks in *Iphigénie* could quite conveniently be taken for courtiers. The knowledge that our actors are required to possess to-day seemed at that time out of place or useless. And it is precisely because our age and our public show themselves to be more exacting and more ready to ridicule an actor who is feebly endowed with the historic sense that the professional making of the actor requires infinitely more labour.

Consequently the actor must become familiar with the entire past of humanity—and be it said that these researches must not be superficial. What is expected of him is not only a clear conception of the facts and of the men, it is the spiritual content of the manners, the customs, and the passions of different peoples and of different times. It is certain that love does not reveal itself in every age in the same forms, and that the expressions of hate vary from century to century, and from people to people. Moreover, different social groups have their proper characteristics, and just as Molière did not ascribe the same language to Alceste as to Mascarille, to Elvire as to Dorine, so the attitudes, the gestures, and all the mannerisms of the actor must reflect with exactitude the sentiments of the characters. Now how can these sentiments be embodied without dipping into books—for the past—and into the great current of life—for the present, in order to gather the data, which are to be co-ordinated and systematized, and harmoniously fused in mimicry, in delivery, and in the general representation of character ?

Thus from the outset nothing seems more difficult or more laborious than the creation of a part. It is not given to everybody to play the part of an emperor, or a workman, a great lady of the *ancien régime* or of the fashionable world, and no doubt a hasty preparation, immediately before the first performance, would only have an absurdly precarious value. Nothing short of a thorough grounding in his subjects, such as will enable him to draw upon all his resources at a specified moment, and will plunge him in the full personality of the character he is impersonating, of the times through which he moves, will enable the interpreter to rise to the height of all his obligations.

The actor must be—if not a scholar or a learned man—at least what used to be called " an all-round man," that is, he should not be inferior in the matter of acquired knowledge to the average of mankind. It should be noted that each person belongs to a social stratum, from which he cannot

emerge save for an extraordinary mishap or exceptional good fortune ; that he is as it were chained
there for life.   It is only the actor who passes
from extreme abjection to extreme splendour, from
the direst poverty to the most sumptuous opulence,
from the age of the Greeks to that of the Inquisi-
tion or our own.   He expresses in turn the super-
stition of an Agamemnon, the fanaticism of a
Duke of Alba, or the social anger of a workman
on strike.   But in addition to the information
derived from books, he is constrained to exercise
ceaseless vigilance, and the famous chair of
Molière remains the best of symbols.   Let the
actor be inquisitive about all professions and all
strata of society ; let him strive to educate himself
concerning all the customs of exotic peoples ;
in a word, let him concentrate in his work the
whole of present and the whole of future humanity : the labour is arduous, but its importance
cannot be overestimated.

The Choice of a Part

WHEN the parts of a play are being allotted, the actor is not always free to choose his part, to adapt himself to the character that best suits him. Unless he is peerless and his genius has endowed him with exceptional prerogatives, he is bound to accept the part assigned to him. But so far as his abilities permit, he must try to give an impersonation that is consonant with his resources. If it be true that there are no such things as small parts, that an actor can produce good effects from an ephemeral creation—and that the hierarchy that prevails in life does not obtain on the stage—it behoves each person to study his capabilities, and become acquainted with his strong points and his weak points. He who excels in *Othello* will be deplorable in the *Bourgeois Gentilhomme*. This does not mean that distinction of classes must be maintained intact, that comedy must be separated from tragedy or from drama by an insurmountable barrier, and that one should be a slave to literary categories.

But *Othello* and the *Bourgeois Gentilhomme*
require the exertion of different qualities that
might very well not be combined in the same man.
If the sage's motto " Know thyself " is valuable in
all the conjunctures of life, it has special applica-
tion to the case of the actor.

It is always a mistake to force one's talent, and
to endeavour to assume qualities which cannot
possibly be combined with other qualities of a
totally different nature.   Delivery, stature, expression, and gesture exercise a preponderant influence
upon the success of an actor and the development
of his career.   It would be presumption on his
part to ignore the laws of his nature and the condi-
tions that predispose him to some lines of business,
while forbidding others.   The actor should take
special heed of this warning when calling in the
aid of his will and relying upon the modifications
it is able to effect ; and before accepting this or
that character, he should scrutinize his abilities
closely and ask himself : does it fit me, shall I be
exposed to insurmountable difficulties in attempt-
ing to personify it ?   And here too instruction,
the conception of the historical or social background, and the analysis of the passions to be
expressed are clearly the essential factors.

The Will

WILL power is a fundamental condition of success for every man ; for the actor it is a condition to which all others are subordinate. As this art exacts labour every day, every hour, and every minute, as the resources of the mind have continuously to be exerted upon study or observation, timid, flabby, indecisive, or idle persons are not wanted.

Persons of great natural talent may fail owing to lack of will power. It is by means of will power that delivery is improved, gesture perfected, sensibility stimulated, and the actor grows adequate to his innumerable material obligations. However excellent his native memory might be, it must be developed and made flexible by incessant labour. If he allows himself to be influenced, to be discouraged, to be rebuffed by the first checks; if he does not make prodigious efforts to overcome the vexations inseparable from every walk of life, in order to adapt himself at will to situations and periods, he is marked out for eventual defeat.

May I quote the advice which Madeleine Brohan once gave me upon this subject ? The injustices of workaday life had disgusted me. And I, of whom it may be said that will power has never been wanting, I was discouraged and complained.

" My poor dear," said the great artist, whom I loved dearly, " my poor dear, there is nothing you can do ; you cannot help being original ; you have a dreadful head of hair that is intractable and naturally curly ; your figure is excessively slender ; in your throat you possess a natural harp ; all this renders you a being apart, which constitutes a crime in vulgar eyes. So much for your physical, now for your moral qualities. You cannot conceal your thoughts or stoop to anything. You will have nothing to do with either hypocrisy or compromise, which is a crime in the eyes of society. Under these circumstances, how can you expect not to arouse jealousy, not to wound people's susceptibilities, and not to make them spiteful ? If you despair because of these attacks, you are lost, for you will lack the strength to fight. In this case, I would advise you to brush your hair, to smear it with oil, so as to make it as flat as the hair of the Corsican, and yet no : for Napoleon's hair was so flat that it was counted to him as an original attribute. Say then as flat as

Prudhon's[1] hair. I would also advise you to put on a little flesh and let your voice break occasionally ; then you would not annoy anyone. But if you wish to remain ' yourself ', my dear, prepare to mount on a little pedestal compounded of calumnies, injustices, flatteries, and lies, with the truths as makeweight. When you are on the pedestal, stand firm and cement it by your talent, your work and your kindness. Be determined. All the spiteful people who have unwittingly provided the first materials for the edifice will kick it then, in hopes of destroying it. But if you are determined, they will be powerless. You have the ambitious thirst for fame, my dear Sarah. Nothing but your resolute will will enable you to satisfy it."

This is indeed the truth. In every other profession, once a certain position has been acquired, once a certain routine has been organized, a man may rest a little on his oars. In the theatre, the nervous tension never ceases, physical effort is added to and fused with intellectual effort. To be a good actor, to pursue the career of a Talma, of a Kean, of a Rachel, it is necessary to have a firmly tempered soul, to be surprised at nothing, to resume each minute the laborious task that has barely just been finished.

[1] Prudhon was one of the actors at the Théâtre Français.

To pass in this way from one part to another, to stride across the centuries, to play Brutus after having impersonated Cæsar, or Juliet after having represented Lady Macbeth, to have the thoughts and feelings of numberless individuals and to express them alternately : all this is a weariness likely to break the strongest.   No doubt they are sustained by the enchanting joy of creation ; they came to earth again when impersonating a fresh character ; they live in a world of passions that stimulate their vital force and lift them out of themselves ;—but if will power be not invoked, if in their creation of this or that character, they were not sustained at once by their high artistic conscience and a determination that is proof against everything, they would very often be tempted to stick to the parts already mastered.

Now the actor who lacks the versatility enabling him to adapt himself to every exigency, who does not keep abreast of dramatic literature itself, the man who would restrict himself to the Greek poets, or to Molière, or to Shakespeare—such an one falls short in the performance of his duty.   He should be prepared to throw himself into the most modern fictions and serve them with the fulness of his talent.   Unlike those scholars who always pursue their investigations into the same subject, and whose activities become almost automatic, he must be prepared to sacrifice at any moment the acquired routine, the repose to which he considers himself entitled, in order to plunge into fresh studies. Art is ageless, and the artist must not know age. Not by indolence or by self-indulgence, but by the absolute possession and mastery of his personality will the artist be able to raise himself to the supreme glory of men whose lives are all creation, all labour, and all enthusiasm.

G

Naturalism

GREAT actors have always been judged by the naturalism they exhibit in their acting. Fidelity to the truth does not always distinguish in our present-day art, and the public will not tolerate a glossing over of reality. The conventions and affected behaviour that might have been admissible at certain periods would certainly not be acceptable at the present time. In this respect dramatic art has made remarkable progress in the course of the last century. But what do we mean by naturalism ? Just as literary or pictorial art will suppress certain objects which could not be exhibited to the eyes of the reader or visitor, so the actor must not shock the modesty of those who listen to him. All art whatsoever presupposes enlightened selection, and no purpose is served by being brutally natural. What it behoves the artist to do, and what is expected of him, is that, in observing the minimum of propriety, he should exhibit the feelings that are supposed to animate him, in the manner they are exhibited in real life by average men amongst his contemporaries. And here must be emphasized once again the necessity of profound study. To be natural does

not mean that an actor should exhibit the passions
in the manner they are exhibited by everybody and
under all circumstances in his epoch.   Just as the
actor is bound, in order to perfect his acting, to be
thoroughly acquainted with the character, so he
must realize that the degree of sensibility is not
invariable in all centuries and in all places.   The
sorrow of old Horace may not be expressed in the
same way as that of the Miser whose cash-box has
been stolen.   The fury of vengeance does not
assume the same aspect with Othello as with a
husband in modern comedy who has discovered
the treachery of his wife.   Thus naturalism is
inseparable from study.   But what is indisput-
able is that naturalism involves qualities that are
anterior to all study, innate qualities of various
kinds.   He who is incapable of feeling strong
passions, of being shaken by anger, of living in
every sense of the word will never be a good actor;
but this brings me to the subject of individual
impersonation, to which I shall return later.

If you would be natural, you must avoid the
persistent mannerisms that actors frequently
adopt, believing they please the public.   In the
end these become merely bad habits.   You must
avoid stiff and chronic poses in order to fit into the
innumerable vicissitudes of existence ; you must
grasp the social position of each character so as to

place it in the proper setting. Each class or category of men is different from the next class or category. The spectator must discover his typical manners on the stage and be able to recognize them at first glance. But the true actor specially distinguishes himself in the great crises of passion. There is no one way of representing affliction, or expressing the extremity of anger. Nothing is more distasteful than to act according to a formula that is constantly repeated ; to have a laugh ready to be adapted to all characters or a manner of dying which will persist in every dramatic fiction. Nature which has not made two beings alike requires incessant diversity. It is true that the more one attempts to define what is natural, the more one perceives the difficulty of squeezing it into a brief and simple formula. For centuries and centuries artists of every class have discussed this serious problem. But in any case, it is possible and permissible to set up a criterion, which may be arbitrary, but is none the less valuable. When a popular audience is moved to tears by the anguish of the actor, when forgetting theatrical convention it imagines that it is present at a real drama, the actor will know that he has achieved the object of his art : he may pride himself on having been natural, for it is never by employing mannerisms that he can plunge an audience into emotion.

Sensibility

A N actor cannot be natural unless he really has power to project his personality. He must in a way forget himself, and divest himself of his proper attributes in order to assume those of his part. He must forget the emotion of the moment, the joy or the sorrow born of the events of the day. And it is because I did not pay sufficient attention to this obligation that I spoilt, as Sarcey told me, one of my appearances at the Comédie Française.

From the stage I had seen my mother, who was very ill from heart trouble, leave her box hurriedly. In witnessing her departure I had an idea that she was about to be attacked by one of those crises which put her life in danger. During the whole of the first act (we were playing *Mademoiselle de Belle-Isle*) I could do no more than ejaculate the words one after the other and stammer the sentences without understanding their meaning.

The public cannot conceive of the tortures endured by the poor actors who are there before them in flesh and blood, gesticulating and uttering phrases, while their hearts, torn with anguish, are with a beloved absent one who is suffering.

The actor must leave behind him the cares and vexations of life, throw aside his personality for several hours, and move in the dream of another life, forgetting everything. But can he do so when a beloved relative is tossing on a bed of suffering ?   Anguish distracts the brain that is living two lives, and makes the heart beat as though it would burst.

My friend Madame Guérard was in the secret. The public not aware of what was happening commenced to fidget. This was a matter of complete indifference to me, as I was thinking of other things. I repeated the words of Mademoiselle de Belle-Isle—a stupid and tiresome part—but I, Sarah, was awaiting news of my mother, and was on the watch for the return of Madame Guérard, to whom I had said : " Open the door on the O.P. side, as soon as you return, and make a sign like this if Mamma is better, and like that if she is worse."

But I could not remember the sign that was to indicate good news, and when I saw my friend, at the end of the third act, opening the door and moving the head up and down as if to indicate yes, I lost my head completely.

It was during the big scene of the third act : when Mademoiselle de Belle-Isle reproaches the Duc de Richelieu (Bressant) with doing her such irreparable harm. The Duke replied :

" Why did not you tell me that some one was listening to us, that some one was concealed ? "

I exclaimed :

" It is Guérard who is bringing me news."

The public was not given an opportunity to understand, for Bressant went on quickly and saved the situation. I was reassured during the interval, and regained all my composure during the last act. My relative success increased at each succeeding performance and became such that I was accused of having a noisy claque in my pay.

It is nevertheless true that during several acts I had not been able to conceal the fearful anxiety that was rending me, and that I had almost compromised my own success and that of the performance. I had been wanting in strength of character, and had temporarily forgotten one of the first duties of the actress.

If the actor retains his mode of living, of thinking and of behaving throughout the manifold characters that he successively impersonates, he cannot feel the passions of these characters ; and, unless he can enter into the feelings of his heroes, however violent they may be, however cruel and vindictive they may seem, he will never be anything but a bad actor. Coldness will be his portion, and not the impetuous ardour which carries away an audience and which is the hallmark of genius. If he does not really feel the anguish of the betrayed lover or of the dishonoured father, if he does not temporarily escape from the dullness of his existence in order to throw himself wholeheartedly into the most acute crises, he will move nobody. How can he convince another of his emotion, of the sincerity of his passions, if he is unable to convince himself to the point of actually becoming the character that he has to impersonate ?

I cannot forbear repeating here the example of Coquelin, who was insensible to the passions of the dramatic characters that he personated. The public itself remained unmoved, at which Coquelin was most illogically surprised. But he never managed to acquire sensibility.

The artist must be like one of those sounding discs which vibrate to every wind, and are agitated by the slightest breeze. If he is not shaken by anger, and if pity does not move him profoundly, he will appear insipid. The public will remember that it is at the play, that an artificial hero is in front of it, that within an hour or two the play will be over, and that, after quitting the sumptuous decorations, it will be back at its dull fireside. The emotion sought after will not have been captured ; the anticipated resurrection will not have taken place ; the audience that has remained unmoved by the performance of the actor, who can give no artistic pleasure, will rightly complain that it has been cheated.

To be worthy of the name an actor must be capable of a continuous dissection of his personality. Great artists have wept like Juliet or like Andromaque, felt the transports of savage love like Phèdre or Hermione, or suffered the pangs of remorse like Macbeth. Hamlet's frenzy will make the spectators shudder if the actor really feels he is Hamlet. Do not let us delude ourselves that we can wear the vesture of another's soul while preserving our own ; do not let us imagine for a moment that we can create an artificial exterior while maintaining our ordinary feelings intact. The actor cannot divide his personality between himself and his part ; he loses his *ego* during the time he remains on the stage, and thus his consciousness skips from age to age, from one people to another, from one social stratum to another, from one hero to another. What he undertakes is a crushing burden ; the task he essays is almost superhuman if he resolves to accomplish it in all its fulness, and intends to be worthy of his art.

He must vivify the thought of the poet or of the dramatist, who also deserts his age and his *milieu* for the age and the *milieu* of his creations.   When Shakespeare wrote *Othello* or *The Merchant of Venice*, he ceased to be an Englishman of his generation, he had temporarily sloughed off the real man, in order to be imbued with all the passion of a jealous Moor, or all the cupidity of a fanatical miser. He did not merely forget the material or moral preoccupations which worried him a few minutes previously, but he was transported by thought, on the wings of imagination, towards other skies. The quality of imagination, which is the master faculty of the poet, must be assimilated by the actor, through whose mind the most diverse ideas must pass at will, and these ideas must be vivid enough to efface the preceding thoughts, and to summon to their aid all the effective and intellectual resources of the actor.   By virtue of this quality the actor equals the poet in creative power.

THIRD PART

Impressions—Criticisms—Memories.

Poetry

ADVICE from the greatest actor will not impart genius to one who intends to adopt a theatrical career. It is difficult enough to provide him with talent. It would still be necessary to cultivate the innate gifts, to fall back on this or that quality with which nature has endowed the young neophyte, to accentuate one characteristic or minimize another. The rest, that is to say success, is a matter of will, of determination that is proof against discouragement from the manifold obstacles with which the career abounds—determination to reach the first rank, but before all to arrive there through one's faith, one's talent, the radiance shed over one's work, the life which one breathes into the characters to which the genius of poets and of dramatists has given birth.

The function of the Conservatoire is to train tragedians and comedians. Thus, as I have tried to show, the teachers have simply to watch those physical qualities of the neophytes that lend themselves to improvement, that is to say, the voice, pronunciation, and gesture. Perfect delivery only comes from that general perfection which the soul imbues with an emotion which communicates itself to others. No teaching can avail anything against natural defects and physical imperfections, or against the lack of a memory or the absence of a voice. Nor can anything be done to counteract the absence of heart, soul, nerves, and the intelligence necessary to understand parts and the intention of the author.

In short the duty of the teacher is that of a patient guardian who repeats incessantly to those whom he has to supervise the three or four defects of which they must free themselves, e.g. " You open the mouth too much." " You say O instead of A." " You walk badly." And this he must never tire of doing, in order gradually to correct natural habits that are unbecoming on the stage, where everything is pressed into the service of Art. Patience and work, especially patience, are essential. If the sacred fire burns in you, you will succeed. If, on the contrary, you are only looking forward to the pleasures with which your illusions surround the career of an actor, the intoxication of more or less doubtful success, you may one day discover that for which you are seeking—for a few years, a few months, perhaps a few days—

only to lose it most surely after a short lapse of time, and to relapse into laborious obscurity and irreparable failure. And it is most probable that you will not obtain any of the desired pleasures, and will simply vegetate amidst innumerable difficulties.

In the course of my long life I have been able to convince myself of the reality of this inner determination suffused by the light and the warmth of faith in Art and in Life. And when I recall the manifold incidents of my career from the end of my convent days to my world tours, I am sure they must prove instructive to many.

There is no doubt that when I was a girl my soul seemed to be turning towards God and religion, and when my family directed me towards dramatic art, I did not think that I had any vocation. But it is very likely that love of the beautiful and of poetry slumbered beneath my religious and mystic sentiment. This love gradually revealed itself during the slow transformation which my mind underwent. Was it not that which caused me to take such delight in the Thursday evenings at the convent, when the pupils recited fables or verses selected from the poetry of Madame Desbordes-Valmore ? I used always to achieve a great personal success in the *Oreiller d'une petite fille.* These poor little trumpery verses would make me weep at this period. I imagined myself entering an unknown and mysterious world, that of Art.

Rachel I never knew, and the ideal which I formed for myself was suggested by Mademoiselle Maria Favart. I took her for my model. To be like Favart became my dream. I took great pains to imitate her, and I did so with such freedom that I perceived with horror that my idol had a method.

Maria Favart was highly esteemed. The modest and bourgeois charm which emanated from the whole of her distinguished person enchanted the public, although she was badly proportioned. Her head was too large, her bust too long, her legs too short.

She gained a tremendous triumph in the part of Andromaque, the lines of which she repeated in a serious and languid voice. I was particularly struck by one scene. It is that in which Céphise impels Andromaque to wed Pyrrhus. Favart moaned the first lines, and almost terrified by evoking her memories, she raised her tone to the climax of pathos, after which her tears, her anguish and the bitterness of her tragic voice all vanished into a false naturalism which the audience greeted with frantic enthusiasm.

I desired to imitate Favart in this same scene, but it was quite impossible. I could not understand the inner reasons that guided my idol in her interpretation of the despair of Andromaque steeped in the most afflicting recollections of a terrible night.

I employed an artful device and managed to see Maria Favart. Régnier introduced me to Delaunay, and the latter introduced me to the *tragédienne* and explained to her the reason of my visit. I was immediately disillusioned. Favart received me pretentiously rolling her *rs*. She arranged for a young girl to give her the cue, and recited to me the scene in question, in order that " I might the better understand what I wanted to know."

I understood so well that I remained openmouthed, and could neither say thank you nor utter any other sound. Favart took my astonishment as a violent effort of admiration. The veil, however, was torn. My idol was no longer an idol. She was no more than a woman with a large head, an inexpressive look, who interpreted feelings and recited lines in a mechanical fashion, confining herself to the employment of a method which always affected the spectators in the same stupid fashion, and appealed to a gross and ignoble sensibility.

She made me repeat the scene in a trembling voice.

This served no useful purpose. From that day I resolved to form an ideal for myself. I no

H

longer wanted to resemble anyone else, and said :
" I will be myself."

I well knew that the path to this goal would
prove toilsome. I was assiduous, energetic, and
laborious. I never missed a class, not even
Father Elie's deportment class.

Deportment ! Do you know what deportment
is ? The way to walk, to sit, to stand erect, to
make a gesture, with harmony and grace. Yes,
it seems that this can be taught. And poor M.
Elie, all powdered and curled like an old beau and
profusely adorned with lace frills, undertook to
show us how to do it. His instruction was accompanied by passes of the little black stick he always
carried in his hand.

" Now, young ladies," he would say, " throw
the body back, hold up the head, walk on tip-toes.
That's right. One, two, three, march."

And we marched along on tip-toes with heads
up and eyelids drawn over our eyes as we tried to
look down in order to see where we were walking.

We used to march as solemnly as camels. There
was also the question of exits. We learned to
make exits. Our steps were supposed to be
guided by our feelings. We had to reach the door
carelessly, furiously, with dignity, with a languid
or with a hasty step. Then we heard " Enough !
Go ! Not a word ! " For M. Elie would not

allow us to murmur a single word. " Everything," Father Elie used to say, " is in the expression, the gesture, the attitude." And we
would practise the look that meant " Enough,
sir, go."

Finally there was the question of sitting down,
to sit down with dignity, or to fall heavily into a
chair. One method of sitting down was particularly complicated. It was the one that meant " I
am listening, Monsieur ; say what you wish."
We had to put everything into it : the desire to
know what was going to be said to us, the fear of
hearing it, the determination to go away, the will
to stay. But there was more besides. There was
the rebellious way of sitting down, with the body
straight, nostrils dilated, arms rigid ; the sitting
down in dejection, with head hanging and arms
dangling ; and the ironical way of sitting down.
Oh that one ! I remember it so well : body
thrown back, mouth raised on one side, laughter
in the eyes, and imperceptible shrugging of the
shoulders . . .

What labour it was to forget all that the poor
man had exerted himself to teach us. Nothing is
more useless than these deportment classes.

Every person moves according to his proportions, and according to his aptitudes. The gesture must depict the thought, and it is harmonious

or stupid according to whether the actor is intelligent or dull.   What can a woman who is too tall do except stride ?   Women who are very small skip along, those who stoop walk like the Eastern women ;   stout women waddle, short-legged ones trot, and the gawky ones walk like cranes.

Actors or actresses whose arms are too short cannot make a graceful gesture.   The instructions of all the Elies in the world can make no difference, and cannot replace short arms by long arms.   Yet Elie did say one true thing :   that gesture should precede speech.

The Conservatoire has forgotten this, and no longer teaches it.   It ought however to pay attention to this noteworthy observation, which I would improve by saying :   Expression ought to precede gesture, which in its turn precedes speech, the latter being only the formula of thought.

As to this I may quote an example taken from *La Tosca*.   Exhausted by anguish and burning with fever, Tosca stretches her hand to take a glass and moisten her parched lips.   On the table is a knife.   The idea springs to her mind to slay the executioner.   Then her look strays towards him, returns to the knife.   Her mind is freed by the look and the gesture, and she emits the cry :
    " Die ! die !   Dastard ! "
If on seeing the knife the actress seized it im-

mediately and killed the miscreant, uttering the same cry of rage without the preliminary look and gesture, the action would be less striking. The public, whose attention would soon be attracted by a new phase of thought, would only have received an uncritical shock, and would not understand this action. This is why the art of the dramatist and that of the actor are intimately bound together. The actor's art requires most delicate execution, since he is responsible to the great minds who entrust him with their efforts.

The remembrance I have preserved of the lessons of M. Elie concerning deportment and gestures is connected in my mind with an unforgettable recollection of a little adventure that one day greatly embarrassed me. It happened at the Tuileries. Agar and I were to act François Coppée's delightful play *Le Passant*, which we had produced at the Odéon. But before the day of the performance, we had to attend to the installation of certain accessories, and rehearse, on which occasion we were to be presented to the Emperor and the Empress.

After being conducted into a small drawing-room on the ground floor, I was waiting with my friend Madame Guérard and the Comte de Laferrière, who was to make the presentations. The latter left the room in order to apprise His

Majesty of our arrival.   I took advantage of the interval to rehearse my three bows.   I bowed murmuring : Sire . . .   Sire . . .

I did this several times diving into my skirt with downcast eyes.

Sire . . .   Sire . . .   Sire . . .

A stifled laugh interrupted me in the midst of a bow.   I thought Madame Guérard was mocking me, and stood up angrily, but I saw that she too was bent over in a half-circle.   Behind me the Emperor was laughing and softly clapping his hands.

I had been bowing I do not know how many times, correcting my bow, and saying :

" This is too low, this is not low enough.   This is not so bad, is it, Guérard ? "

Had he witnessed all this ?   In spite of my confusion, I managed to bow.   But Napoleon smilingly stopped me.

" It's no good," he said.   " It will never be as pretty as it was just now.   Reserve them for the Empress who awaits you."

The Emperor's remark made me feel very uncomfortable during the whole time of the presentation and the visit.   I remained absent-minded in the presence of the Emperor as well as in that of the Empress.

But nobody is exempt from such misadven-

tures. Did not a little mishap of an almost similar kind befall the Empress herself on leaving that
very performance of *Le Passant* ? I watched it
all through a slit in the curtain. During the performance, the Empress Eugénie, who possessed
extremely pretty little feet, felt her shoe pinching.
One of her heels had prudently slipped out of its
cruel case, leaving the foot covered only at the toe.
When the play was over, it was found impossible
to force the little foot back into its prison. The
Queen of Holland and the Prince of Orange and
an admiring crowd were there ; and their presence added to Her Majesty's embarrassment. A
rampart of generals and orderly officers was necessary before the little imperial rebel could be forced
into the tight shoe. Eventually everything was
in order, and there was general merriment. I
would add, as it concerns the subject of this anecdote, that Agar and I were surrounded, and a
great fuss was made of us. The grace and charm
of the delightful and timid Coppée's poetry was
really the chief cause of this triumph.

It was also because I loved reciting verse above
everything. I prefer it to prose.

I was then at the Odéon. One day of rehearsal,
Chilly, one of the managers (fortunately Duques-
nel was his partner), sought me out and said :

" Your performance is very well, my child, but

it is too apparent that you are reciting verse. You emphasize the pause and the rhyme."

I exclaimed directly :

" But the alexandrine is constructed with two wings to give flight to thought, and the rhymes are difficulties which the poet has overcome. The public must understand and learn them ; it must realize with what ease the poet triumphs over every obstacle . . ."

A voice murmured behind me :

" Ah ! say my verses as you said them just now, and I will kiss the hem of your mantle ! "

Looking round I saw before me a tall young man, pale and slender, his eyes full of tears, who resembled Napoleon, or Brienne. It was François Coppée. I put my arms round his neck.

Ah ! how far I had progressed from the *Oreiller d'une petite fille* ! I no longer recited in a simple and trembling voice, which ignored the subtle music of the mysterious poetry :

> Laisse descendre au soir un ange qui pardonne
> Pour répondre à des voix que l'on entend gémir
> Mets sous l'enfant perdu que la mère abandonne
> Un petit oreiller qui le fera dormir.

At the Conservatoire I passed my first examination in *Zaire*.

" Strike ! " I said, " I love him."

In spite of Provost, I had fallen at the feet of

Nerestan with a genuine sob, arms outstretched, offering my heart full of love to the mortal stroke that I awaited, and I had murmured this " Strike ! " . . . tenderly, and not vehemently.

I had been coached for my second examination (Tragedy and Comedy) by Casimir Delavigne. I had to recite verse, but it was not poetry. Shortly afterwards I secured an engagement at the Comédie Française, where I made my debut in Racine's *Iphigénie*. Then I appeared in *Les Femmes Savantes*, when I scored a real success, which attracted attention to me. Moreover, it was that play and my part of Henriette which was the indirect cause of my leaving the Comédie Française. Madame Nathalie, an illustrious shareholder who played the part of Philaminte, and who was the most ill-natured of women, mercilessly ridiculed me because I was a young beginner, and continued to scold me so harshly that at length I soundly boxed her ears. There was a great scandal, and on being asked for an apology, I tendered my resignation.

I secured an engagement at the Odéon, where I declaimed the verse of Racine in the part of young Zacharie, in *Athalie*, and the verse of François Coppée in *Le Passant*. I scored a great success in these rôles. I was Zanette, and was intoxicated by the harmony, the exquisite rhythm, and

the poetry of this rôle. And I listened to my own
voice as it poured forth to reach the anxious attention of the public and waft it away to share in the
melancholy and charming beauty of this delightful
art.

Je veux un souvenir, et non pas une aumône
Un rien, mais qui soit bien à vous—Tenez je veux
La triste fleur qui meurt dans vos sombres cheveux.

It must be avowed that the Odéon is a newer
and more stimulating sanctuary for art than the
Comédie Française. At the Odéon we only
breathed dreams; we did not walk; we hovered
with wings. What a difference there was between
the actors, as well as between the audiences of
these two theatres. The solemn actors at the
Comédie had reached the end of their efforts.
What use exerting themselves further ? The
public, which consisted of old subscribers, did not
ask much, and were satisfied with the respect paid
to traditions. Oh those traditions ! How many
enthusiastic and sincere actors have found themselves fettered by them. I well remember all the
faults that were imputed to me when I played
Phèdre for the first time at the Comédie Française. There were traditions which one could not
resist under pain of being broken. There were
others less terrible. A funny little incident comes
into my mind. An old shareholder (he was a pro-

fessor at the Sorbonne) sought me out and told me curtly :

"Mademoiselle, it signifies a want of respect to turn your back on the public ! "

"But, Monsieur, I was leading an old lady off the stage, I could not very well walk with her backwards."

"Actresses who have preceded you, Mademoiselle, and who have as much talent as you, if not more, found a way of crossing the stage without turning their backs on the public."

And he turned sharply on his heels. I hastened to detain him.

"Excuse me, Monsieur . . . will you go to that door, through which you intended to pass, without turning your back on me ? "

He made an attempt, but boiling over with wrath, he left me turning his back and slamming the door.

There are also moral traditions which approach the legendary. I have sometimes tried, in concert with an author, to compel the public to return to the truth and to abolish the legendary side of certain characters that present-day history represents to us as they were in reality. The public has not followed my lead. And I have quickly been obliged to recognize that the legend remains victorious in spite of history, and that it is preferable

to surrender to it.   What was Joan of Arc ?   Was
she a robust peasant girl, a buxom wench exposed
to the promiscuities of her barbarous age among
the soldiers who were not sparing of their jokes ?
No—she was a frail being led by a divine soul.
An invisible angel supported her arm which carried the heavy sword.   It is the legend that interests us.   We have fashioned it to our own desires.
It remains triumphant.

Since these far-off times to which I have alluded,
I have interpreted many other works of the poets.
None is dearer to me than those of the wonderful
Edmond Rostand.   But there is no doubt that I
could not have played *l'Aiglon* in the way I did if
I had been at the commencement of my career.
I have had to follow a slow process of evolution,
learning, learning, and always learning in continuously renewed contact with the works that
have come my way.   I have assimilated the manifold technique of the dramatists who have followed
each other in the passage of years like the waves
of the sea.   And I have myself unconsciously
created a personal technique, in order to heighten
the sonorous music of verse, the melody of words,
and the music and the melody of thought.

Why I could not play Corneille

AFTER the performance of *Le Passant* that we gave at the Tuileries, the Emperor Napoleon came to congratulate Agar and myself in the little saloon that had been reserved for us. He paid his compliments with charming grace.

" I shall soon be playing Camille in Corneille's *Horace*," said Agar. " I should be most delighted if your Majesty would deign to honour this performance by your presence."

" Very well," answered the sovereign : " I will go to see you, although I prefer Racine."

I could have hugged him for this sentiment, as I too prefer Racine.

Truly I prefer Racine, and have never played Corneille. I have tried—for my own satisfaction —and have gladly abandoned the attempt. I have often been asked why I have such a predilection for Racine, and such a horror of Corneille. The explanation is simple : in my opinion Corneille, the sublime Corneille, does not know how to make a woman talk. None of his heroines (Psyche must be excepted) is really a woman. They declaim, but their heart is not in their breast, it beats in their head. Their love is of a subtle, complicated, and hair-splitting variety.

Many people, in particular M. Perrin, the director of the Comédie Française, and my comrade Mounet-Sully, have implored me to put this antipathy aside. I consented to play Chimène, the heroine of the *Cid*, more than twenty times. And more than twenty times I retracted my consent. I could not interpret a character so false, so changeable, so defective in humanity.

I find Corneille often superhuman, but never human. I may be a novice in dramatic criticism, but I have a clear idea of the female parts of Corneille from the standpoint of their interpretation by women. It is a woman who interprets Camille, who plays Chimène ; and these parts ought to give scope for feminine sentiments. To my way of thinking, they do nothing of the kind.

Chimène is an odious and pretentious creature. When she learns of the quarrel of her father with the father of Rodrigue, her betrothed, she exclaims :

Mon cœur outré d'ennuis n'ose rien espérer
Un orage si prompt qui trouble une bonace
D'un naufrage certain nous porte la menace
Je n'en saurais douter je péris dans le port.

Ah, this " heart strained with sorrows " makes
me shudder, and this great love (the calm) men-
aced by the quarrel of the two fathers (the storm)
which will cause the shipwreck of the two lovers ;
and which will lead to her " shipwreck even in
harbour . . .''

All this is heavy, ludicrous, far-fetched, and
commonplace. Then when she learns of the
death of her father slain by her lover, she throws
herself at the feet of the king and cries :

> D'un jeune audacieux punissez l'insolence. . .
> (Punish the presumption of an audacious youth.)

Does genuine sorrow utter itself in this fashion ?
She proceeds to describe her sorrow in this florid
manner for a dozen lines, after which she falls
down exhausted. The king beholds her crushed
and speechless, and consoles her gently. And
the poor crushed woman suddenly recovers her
voice, gets up and shows herself a veritable fury.
During her long monologue Chimène does not
utter one fitting phrase : she invokes the wounds
of her father which she represents as a mouth
imploring vengeance, after having said that the
blood which flowed from the side traced her duty
in the dust. Then she suggests to the king that
if he does not punish the daring young man, he
will extinguish the ardour to serve him in the
hearts of all those who surround him. It is there-

fore for the king's interest, and not for her own vengeance, that she demands the head of her lover.

She seems to me to be without naturalness, without movement, and without love ; and in spite of my good will, I have been unable to discover in myself sufficient talent and emotion to personate this sorrow.

In the third act the metaphor becomes almost unintelligible.   Chimène says to Elvire :

> Pleurez, pleurez, mes yeux, et fondez-vous en eau.
> La moitié de ma vie a mis l'autre au tombeau
> Et m'oblige   venger, après ce coup funeste
> Celle que je n'ai plus par celle qui me reste.[1]

This approaches the ridiculous, and Chimène seems to me no more than a caviller without fever and without passion.   Moreover, during the entire play she is haunted by her " glory." She talks too much of glory and not enough of love.   There is neither love nor sorrow in her. This Chimène only resembles a woman in her inconsistency, and because she never knows what she wants.   This is not enough to encourage me

---

[1] Weep, weep, mine eyes and dissolve yourself in tears.   The one half of my life (i.e. Rodrigo) has laid the other half (i.e. my father) in the grave, and compels me to revenge, after this fatal blow, that which I have no more (i.e. my father) on that which still remains to me (i.e. Rodrigo).

to recite the logical lines which Corneille has written for her.

And what of Camille, that other heroine, the fiancée of Curiace ?

She discusses with Julie the meaning of the dream she has had, then believing that Curiace has basely run away from the battle for love of her, she thanks him for doing so ; but she quibbles about what her father will say and tells her fiancé Curiace :

> Mais as-tu vu mon père, et peut-il endurer
> Qu'ainsi dans sa maison tu t'oses retirer ?
> Ne préfère-t-il point l'Etat à sa famille
> Ne regarde-t-il point Rome plus que sa fille ? etc.[1]

And when Curiace rightly repudiates the sentiment of cowardice imputed to him by his mistress, and informs her by what sudden turn the battle between the Albine and Roman peoples has been transformed into a duel between heroes chosen by both camps, Camille cries :

> O Dieux, que ce discours rend mon âme contente.

This is all she can find to say. When later she learns that he has been chosen as a combatant, she urges him to be a coward, and goes on dis-

---

[1] But hast thou seen him, father ?   And can he suffer that thus into his house thou darest to appear ?   Does he not prefer the State to his family ?   Does he not think more of Rome than of his daughter ?

I

cussing with stupid pathos, hoping without hope, and weeping without tears, until the moment she hears that Curiace has been killed by her brother Horace. She has only one word for this :

" Alas ! "

Yes, this is all she can find to say after listening to the most endless of recitals, and at the same time the most sorrowful for her love. She does not flee in order to yield herself to her sorrow. No. She stays there, while old Horace and Valère congratulate each other. And when they have gone, having no further partner for a new discussion, she recounts her misfortunes to the public who are there to listen to them. And she meanders on through fifty-six lines. Finally seeing Horace approach, she murmurs :

> Il vient : préparons-nous à montrer constamment
> Ce que doit une amante à la mort d'un amant.[1]

In this way she deliberately works herself up to a crisis of hysterical fury, which would be justified if it were spontaneous. She is not moved by what she is suffering, but by her desire to displease her brother. She says as much in her soliloquy :

> Et prenons, s'il se peut, plaisir à lui deplaire.

[1] He comes—let me prepare to show firmly what a woman owes to the death of a lover.

In fact, she succeeds in angering him to such an extent that he kills her.

I grant that Camille's invocation :

> Rome, l'unique object de mon ressentiment
> Rome à qui vient ton bras d'immoler mon amant

is a superb outburst, but it is that of a Fury, and not of a despairing lover.

The budding *tragédiennes* of the Conservatoire often select this piece for their examination, and they are not wrong. It is a passage most suitable to produce an effect.

I have studied—not at the Conservatoire, when I was too young and too feeble of voice for this study—but since those days I have studied Camille. I even promised Perrin to play this part, but the more I studied Camille, the more I hated her.

One of our greatest poets, Catulle Mendès, was enamoured of Corneille. He undertook to cure me of my aversion for Corneille's heroines. He brought to his task contagious enthusiasm, persuasive skill, and a thorough knowledge of our classics, but he effected no result.

Is it my profound love for Racine's women ? Is it my artistic nature which cannot lend itself to these heavy and pompous lines ? I do not know. But after learning and thoroughly studying Chimène, Camille and Pauline, of *Polyeucte*, I renounced Corneille for ever.

Ah! this Pauline, who commences like a provincial suffragette :

> Tu vois, ma Stratonice, en quel siècle nous sommes :
> Voilà notre pouvoir sur les esprits des hommes.

It is not a woman, but an advocate. Like the other heroines of Corneille, she argues and quibbles with Sevère, whom she loves always, while she only loves Polyeucte by obedience ; with her father, who reproaches her with this obedience, and would like to see her rebel. She is devoid of heart.

Nothing tires me more than the study of Corneille's female characters. I break off continually and spend hours seeking the reason for the sudden changes in their hearts. And in the end I feel convinced that their hearts do not exist at all.

The heroines of Corneille are nothing more than minds which differ from the minds of men by the instability of their sentiments and the abrupt changes in the manifestation of their love.

They are distinguished from men by their hysteria. They are hysterical quibblers.

How remote they are from the women of Racine, who still remain women however heroic their feelings. Racine and Corneille both treated the same subject : *Bérénice*. How far apart these

two women are ! Both love Titus, and both
express their anguish at having to separate, for
political reasons, from that Emperor of whom
Rome exacts marriage with a Roman woman and
not with Bérénice, Queen of Palestine.

Take Corneille's woman : she only thinks of
" what people will say." It is only her pride
that is at stake. It is not a question of love,
but of precedence. An odious attitude. At the
moment of breaking for ever the ties that have
bound her and Titus together for five years, in a
perpetual hope of definite union, she can only
utter a bombastic and involved apostrophe.

Listen to the Bérénice of Racine :

Dans un mois, dans un an, comment souffrirons-nous,
Seigneur, que tant de mers me separent de vous,
Que le jour recommence et que le jour finisse
Sans que jamais Titus puisse voir Bérénice,
Sans que de tout le jour je puisse voir Titus ? [1]

This is sorrow gracefully expressed. What a
woman this Bérénice is ! She tries to dissimulate
her feelings under reproaches. She wants to

[1] A month will come, a year will come, and we—
We shall be parted by a world of seas.
How shall we suffer when the day begins
And the sun climbs the sky and then declines
And Titus will not see his Bérénice
And all the day she will not look on Titus.
(*John Masefield's translation.*)

hide her anguish ; but the word " good-bye "
tears her heart, she cannot say more.

The women of Racine are the women of every
age, from the birth of the world until the present
time.   They are those who will arise to-morrow,
who will be born continually.

Need I speak of Phèdre !   Is not she the most
appealing, the purest, the most unfortunate victim
of love ?   *She* does not attempt to split hairs.
As soon as she sees Hippolyte, she seizes the
hand of her nurse, and placing it on her heart,
murmurs, almost overcome with emotion :

> Le voici :   vers mon cœur tout mon sang se retire.
> J'oublie en le voyant, ce que je viens lui dire.

What simplicity of utterance !   It might be a
woman of to-day who is speaking :

> Le voici . . . Sens, comme mon cœur bat fort . . .

A woman of the people would exclaim : " Ah !
bon Dieu ! le voici :   mon sang n'a fait qu'un
tour ! "

And what a masterpiece is Phèdre's declara-
tion !   She is pleading for her son.   She knows
Hippolyte to be loyal, and begs his support; and
the eleven lines that follow contain everything
that can be said.   She implores support for her
son, while announcing her own approaching
death, which will have the effect of making

Hippolyte's task easier. She stimulates the latter's courage. And she confesses to him her fear of having, by her own behaviour, closed to pity that generous heart. And how human is her defence !

Dans le fond de mon cœur vous ne pouvez lire.

This is the commencement of the avowal, but she will not tell her secret ; she does not want to tell it. It escapes from her in her cry of revolt against the gods.

Ah ! Seigneur ! Que le ciel, j'ose ici l'attester,
De cette loi commune a voulu m'excepter
Qu'un mal bien different me trouble et me dévore !

In saying more than she intended, she has betrayed herself. A more experienced man would have understood her cry of despair, but Hippolyte unwittingly furnishes her with arguments which will insensibly lead her to confession. And gradually, hypnotized by the present reality of the dream which has haunted her every hour of her life for months, she loses consciousness of people and places; she speaks like a somnambulist; and repeats aloud all that she has murmured during her agonies of insomnia. Hippolyte's exclamation recalls her to herself ; she stammers. And beside herself with shame and wounded, she cries out the truth, and asks for death at the hand of him whom she has offended while adoring him.

All this is love, and anguish, and life with its eternal blemish.

I never saw Rachel, but I understand she was admirable in *Phèdre*. I have seen other *tragédiennes* in this part, and have never been able to understand why they interpreted Phèdre as a termagant, or a neurotic fury.

For the rest, I have noticed that artists who excel in Corneille are bad interpreters of Racine. Exception must doubtless be made of Rachel, who, it seems, was as wonderful in personating the heroines of Racine as those of Corneille.

Perhaps those who will read these lines will understand the principles that have guided me when I played the characters of Racine. I have tried to assimilate the mysterious charm of the pure and touching art of Racine, to render it more obvious to the public that is too apt to find in these tragedies nothing but school remembrances.

Why I have played Male Parts

I HAVE often been asked why I am so fond
of playing male parts, and in particular why
I prefer the part of Hamlet to that of
Ophelia. As a matter of fact, it is not male
parts, but male brains that I prefer, and among
all the characters, that of Hamlet has attracted
me because it is the most original, the most subtle,
the most tortuous, and yet the most simple for
the unity of his dream.

This being who appears to be so complex has
only one idea : to avenge his father. It is true
that this idea is divided into two parts : first of
all, is it certain that the death of his father was
the result of a crime ? Further, is not this drama
and the circumstances that surround it the work
of the Evil One ?

It is around this primary uncertainty that
revolve continually the suspicions, the inquietudes,
the remorse, and the terrors of being the puppet
of a malignant spirit. When his father appears
to him, Hamlet still suspects the malign spirit

that appears as a beloved relative in order to deceive the better. And we observe him discussing the most painful alternatives.

By some it is affirmed that Hamlet is mad. For my part I decline to accept this view. I find him the most sensible, the most artful, but the most unhappy of men. He tortures himself ; he discovers himself a coward, and yet the fear of being a plaything of the infernal powers obsesses him. He discusses with himself, elaborates a plan which will ease his conscience ; he proceeds to arrange the details of a play representing the assassination of his father such as it was recounted to him by the latter's shade. All this is the conduct of a very sensible person, of a thinker, and not of a madman.

In the famous monologue : To be or not to be—Hamlet reveals himself completely. His life is a burden, and yet he does not kill himself. His marshalling of all the doubts is heartrending. How he suffers to see the mother he loves as the loving wife of his father's assassin ! He struggles with all the thoughts that crowd thick upon him. And all the psychology of Hamlet's character is revealed to us by himself.

The fact that Hamlet arranges with great skill his plan of investigation into the conscience of the king his uncle is ample evidence that he is

in his right mind. And when at length he is
persuaded that the latter is his father's assassin,
what intense joy surges through him at the idea
of being free. The uncertainty had stifled the
explosion of his vengeance. Now he is free, and
will be able to avenge his father.

It is unquestionably a great delight for an artist
to be able to interpret such a complex character.
It had been my desire for many years to play
Hamlet, and I was unable to decide to do so
until I read the admirable translation by Marcel
Schwob. I have played Ophelia in the Hamlet
of Cressonnois, but Ophelia brought nothing new
to me in the study of character.

A very learned Englishman, who was also a
great Shakespearian enthusiast, once asked me
who had initiated me into this mysterious Hamlet.
" Why . . . himself ! " I replied. " Every
time that Hamlet finds himself alone and reveals
the depths of his mysterious soul."

Generally speaking male parts are more intellectual than female parts. This is the secret of
my preference. No female character has opened
up a field so large for the exploration of sensations
and human sorrows as that of Hamlet. Phèdre
alone has afforded me the charm of prying into a
heart that is really afflicted.

I am able to say that I have had the rare, and

I believe unique, opportunity of playing three
Hamlets : the black Hamlet of Shakespeare :
l'Aiglon, the white Hamlet of Rostand, and
Lorenzaccio, the Florentine Hamlet of Alfred de
Musset.

Both Hamlet and the duc de Reichstadt have
a soul that has been outraged by an unworthy
mother. Civilization has toned down the demands of Napoleon's son. As Hamlet indulges
in raillery with Horatio, so l'Aiglon chaffs his
teacher : " Is he a prisoner ? Oh no . . . but
. . ." In the two Hamlets, the white and the
black, there is the same scene between mother
and son. With Shakespeare a coarse scene,
terrifying in its truth and savagery. In Rostand, the words are well chosen, civilization has
moderated the anger, the sarcasm is clothed with
courtesy, but the anguish remains the same. I
have been passionately fond of these two Hamlets.

The third, Lorenzaccio, is less pure. The
means which he employs to achieve his object
are dishonourable, but this was not unusual under
the Renaissance. Shakespeare's Hamlet rejects
daggers, traps, and poisons. Rostand's Hamlet
is tied by the invisible threads of politics ; the
more he tries to break loose from them, the more
they fetter him.

Musset's Hamlet wallows in intrigues, orgies,

and sumptuous luxury ; but he has, in the depths of his soul, a tiny flame that at times illumines his whole being. It is not a father assassinated, a father betrayed, that he is called upon to avenge : it is a mother butchered, and that mother is his country. He allows himself to be insulted and treated as a coward in order to gain his ends. He discloses the real nature of his soul to Philippe Strozzi, the most honest among honest men. He opens the floodgates of his lacerated heart in a magnificent flight of words. And this pleading is of incomparable power. I tremble all over when I become the interpreter of the poet. In no female character am I able to discover such a variety of emotions, such a compelling power.

Many are the male parts that I should have liked to play. And among them are Mephistopheles and l'Avare. But a woman can only interpret a male part when it represents a mind in a feeble body. A woman would not be able to play Napoleon, Don Juan, or Romeo.

Mephistopheles . . . yes, because this character is in reality a fallen angel, the malign spirit that accompanies Faust. He is not a real man of flesh and blood. I have witnessed Hamlet played abroad by several tragedians, and I have always been struck by the contrast between the mental fever and the physical vigour of him I have seen act.

These tragedians seemed to me in too splendid
health, with muscles too solid to lend credence
to so much despairing insomnia, so much in-
ward strife.   The pain that gnaws at this unhappy
Hamlet would not leave him with fine calves, a
plump stomach, a splendid pair of shoulders.   I
know that, thanks to powder, the complexion is
pale ; that, thanks to burnt cork, the eye is ringed,
but the fine healthy appearance of the rest of the
body gives the lie to that wasted countenance.

Hamlet, l'Aiglon, and Lorenzaccio are minds
haunted by doubt and despair, hearts that are
beating ever more strongly and ceaselessly tortured by the dreams they conjure up.   The soul
frets the body.   When seeing and hearing these
Hamlets on the stage, the spectator should receive
the impression that the fiery soul is always threat-
ening to burst its tenement of clay.   The artist
must be divested of all virility.   He must make
us see a phantom compounded of the atoms of
life and of the decay that leads to death.   It is a
brain ceaselessly warring against the reality of
things.   It is a soul that longs to escape from
its carnal vestment.   That is why I claim that
these parts always gain when they are played by
intellectual women, who alone are able to pre-
serve their character of unsexed beings, and their
perfume of mystery.

If I had been a man, it seems to me that I should have had such a splendid career ! At the theatre the parts designed for men are always the finest. And yet it is the only art where women may sometimes prove superior to men.

The great feminine painters, Rosa Bonheur, Madeleine Lemaire, Mme. Dermont-Breton, Louise Abbema, Maud Earle, have manifested varying degrees of real talent. But none of them approaches Raphael, Leonardo da Vinci, Rubens, Velasquez, Delacroix, Edouard Detaille, Alfred Stevens, Bastien Lepage. In music no woman had an opportunity of producing an opera before Augusta Holmes ; Cecile Chaminade is a skilful pianist and a composer of great talent : but neither of these women approaches Bach, Mozart, Beethoven, Wagner, Schumann, Gounod, Massenet, Saint-Saens. In poetry Mmes. Desbordes-Valmore, Ackermann, de Noailles, Lucie Delarue-Mardrus, Rosemonde Gerard, de Régnier, Helene Picard, Jane Catulle Mendès, all have excellent talent, but they are a long way from Ronsard, Racine, Victor Hugo, Lamartine, Musset, Edmond Rostand, Jean Richepin, and so many other illustrious names.

I will not mention sculpture, as there is no woman who is really a great sculptor.

On the other hand, in the theatre the great female artists are more numerous than the men. We know that Nero was a great actor ; but Theodora was a greater than he : Roscius was, it seems, an illustrious actor, and the poor man paid very dearly for his celebrity.

But for two centuries the number of women artists who have adorned the French stage has surpassed the number of men artists. We have only Baron, Talma, and Mounet Sully to put against Mlle. Duclos, Adrienne Lecouvreur, Clairon, la Champmesle, Mlle. Georges, Mlle. Mars, and Rachel. And this seems to me to accord with the fitness of things.

The dramatic art would appear to be rather a feminine art ; it contains in itself all the artifices which belong to the province of woman : the desire to please, facility to express emotions and hide defects, and the faculty of assimilation which is the real essence of woman. And what still more endows woman with a slight superiority is the fact that she is woman, and that her physical qualities generally prevail over the physical qualities of man. This is the reason why our art, which is so fine and so complete because it reflects all other arts, remains on a slightly inferior plane, because it cannot be practised without beauty of form or face.

The Actor and the Public

THE relations of the actor to the public do not always depend upon the amount of talent expended. There are actors devoid of talent who are very successful, and, on the other hand, there are others equipped with knowledge and technical skill who cannot emerge from obscurity. In this connection I always think of the prize carried off at the Conservatoire by my comrade Marie Lloyd. In spite of her monotonous delivery, her careless enunciation, and the impersonality of her acting, she gained the votes. It was because she was tall, with delicate white shoulders emerging modestly from her low dress. Her large brown eyes shone with dilated pupils. Her small full mouth would give a sly little smile at the corners, her wonderfully shaped nose had quivering nostrils, and the oval of her beautiful face was intercepted by two little pearly, transparent ears of the most exquisite shape. A long, flexible white neck supported this charming head. It was really a beauty prize that the jury had conscientiously awarded to Marie Lloyd. Laughing and radiant, she had appeared in Célimène, her examination piece. And although she possessed no talent, she proved to be the personification of Célimène. Without effort, she revealed herself as the embodiment of a coquette, a coquette of twenty unconsciously cruel.

An actor who personates a character for which he seems to have been born is bound to be a success. The imperfections of his acting pass unperceived, and the spectator's whole attention is attracted by the personality that emerges from the comedian's acting. But if the latter confines himself to following the same line of business, however perfect he may show himself to be, the public will tire of always seeing him with the same smiles, the same gestures, and the same inflexions.

It is obvious that the psychical activity of the actor who constructs on the stage a personality superimposed on his own, will influence more or less strongly the collective sensibility of the public. In the same way the collective mentality of the coadjutors will influence favourably or unfavourably the animating energy of the actor. The mechanism of this double exchange of influences functions in a mysterious fashion, and I will not attempt to analyse here the imponderable elements that come into play. I will confine myself to setting down what has transpired in my personal experience.

Now I suffer from terrible stage fright. When I was a beginner, I was afflicted with timidity, but not with stage fright. I sometimes became as red as a turkeycock when my gaze met that of a spectator ; I felt ashamed at speaking so loudly before so many silent people. This was the result of my convent education ; but I felt no sensation of fear.

The first time that I experienced a real sensation of fright was in the month of January, 1869, at the seventh or eighth performance of *Le Passant*. The success of this little masterpiece had been colossal, and my interpretation had charmed the public, especially the students.

When I made my entry on this particular day, I was suddenly acclaimed. I looked towards the Imperial box, thinking the Emperor had just entered the theatre. But the box was empty, and I could only conclude that all this applause was for me. I was seized with a nervous trembling, and a strong desire to weep caused my eyes to smart.

That evening I gained an enormous success. And yet the doubt persisted in me. Shall I have sufficient talent to be the Star they are looking for ? I wondered. From that day I was dominated by fear, and a martyr to stage fright.

There is the stage fright that paralyses and the stage fright that maddens. The latter kind is to be preferred as an alternative. It makes one do too much, but at any rate one does something. I owe it to this type of stage fright that I gained one of my greatest successes in England, in a performance of *Phèdre*. At the commencement of the performance the idea occurred to me : suppose I should forget what I have to say ? And no longer mistress of myself, I began my performance on a note that was a little too high. Once I was launched, it was impossible to pitch my voice lower. I suffered, wept, implored, cried. Yes, my suffering was real enough. I was as if possessed by a god. When the curtain went down, I fell swooning, and Mounet Sully raised me inanimate and carried me to my dressing-room. I returned, however, to make a frenzied bow to the public, who, ignorant of what had taken place, were calling for me with loud cries. An ovation was accorded me that was unique (as John Murray stated in the *Gaulois*) in the annals of the English theatre.

Ah, success ! With what a strong chain it rivets one, and how painful it sometimes is. How many times the noise made around me, the good said in my favour, the bad written against me, have invaded my tranquillity and created an atmosphere of battle. Jealous friends, secret or open enemies, into what turmoil have you not often thrust me! And how many times have I not been accused of an immoderate liking for advertisement.

The public imagine that the noise made about famous artists is deliberately provoked by these artists themselves, in their anxiety to see their names cropping up continually under all sorts of pretexts.

Alas, we are the victims of advertisement. Those who taste the joys and sorrows of fame when they have passed forty, know how to look after themselves. They know what is concealed beneath the flowers, and what the gossip, the calumnies, and the praise are worth. But as for those who win fame when they are twenty, they know nothing, and are caught up in the whirlpool.

As for me, my first title to advertisement was my extraordinary slimness and my fragile health. I had scarcely begun before epigrams, puns, and caricatures were indulged in to the heart's content.

Was it really for advertising purposes that I

was so slender, so thin, and so weak, that I spent six months in bed, racked with illness ? My name became famous before I did.

As would be expected, different publics react in different ways to our art. For my part, I have always taken great delight in acting before foreign publics. For very many years I have been in the habit of carrying the French language to the ends of the earth. I have been in every European country, in the two Americas, and in Australia.

Several French artists had toured Europe before me. Generally speaking, the public before whom we act French plays in each great European city is the " select " public, that is, the fashionable and diplomatic world, which knows the French language fairly well. I except from this Belgium and Switzerland, where the language is French.

To perform, for example, at Brussels is the same as playing in Paris, and even before a first-night public in Paris. Nothing escapes this public, neither the beauties of our language, nor the subtleties nor the profound philosophy of our great authors, nor the magnificent verse of our classic and present-day poets. The students are the same as ours : noisy, boasting, and enthusiastic. I adore—and all artists are of the same opinion—we adore the Brussels public. The other towns of Belgium are not so completely French as Brussels, but all are very interested in our French art. Antwerp, for example, is a city where the public still maintains considerable enthusiasm for our literary works.

The Italian public is more difficult to conquer. It has little interest in the foreign theatre. At Rome, the audiences manifest courtesy and tact, and relish the new art submitted to them. But Rome is a cosmopolitan city ; all foreigners of eminent distinction, all the artists of every country meet there. A performance given in Rome by a first-class company is an entertainment for the whole of Roman society, and the *impresario* may count upon two or three packed houses. The artist perceives that he is playing before an intellectual and refined public which understands all the finer shades of our language.

Naples is an admirable city for tourists, but odious to artists, especially those who bring with them the great French art.

Italians have a horror of French verse, especially the alexandrine, which they find heavy and pompous. The first time that I played on a tour in Italy, more than thirty years ago, I gave a great farewell performance at Milan. We had been playing at Milan a whole week with very considerable success ; in fact the Milanese public,

together with the public of Rome, is the most
intellectual in Italy. In order to express my
gratitude at the reception that had been accorded
us, I chose what I believed to be the finest jewels
of my repertory. I arranged my programme with
the second act of *Phèdre*, the fifth of *Hernani*,
the fourth of *Rome vaincue*, ending with *Le Passant*. It was a choice designed for cultivated and
literary minds.

The house was packed. A rain of flowers
greeted my entry on the stage ; but the curtain
fell amidst a glacial silence, interrupted by a few
feeble hurrahs and friendly bravos. *Phèdre* met
with the same success, and *Rome vaincue*, in which
I appeared as a blind old woman of ninety, was
not more fortunate. Some friends came to see
me during the intervals and noticed my disappointed expression. They tried to explain to
me that . . . etc. . . .

An eminent Italian, a political writer and a
remarkable orator, approached with outstretched
hands :

" Who is the fool that has arranged your programme ? " he exclaimed. " I can assure you,
my dear friend, that the Italians cannot tolerate
your heavy alexandrines dragging empty carts of
poetry. I hope your last piece is not in verse,
as we want to give you a triumphant ovation,

and we are enervated and bored by these hundreds of lines."

" Ah, very bored," I answered him. " I will change the last piece, as *Le Passant* is also in verse."

" What, more alexandrines ! " he exclaimed in dismay.

" Yes, yes, alexandrines," I retorted, clenching the teeth. " But I will give you another little piece."

" Oh, bless you, my divine one ! I will inform the audience."

Then turning towards me :

" What is the name of the last piece you are going to play ? "

" *Le Départ.* It contains one act, is in prose and fairly short, but charming."

" Bravo ! Bravo ! "

And he withdrew.

When my maid was preparing my costume for *Le Passant,* I murmured to her : " Leave all that, quick, my dress, my mantle, my hat, a carriage."

In leaving I ran across the *impresario,* who did not recognize me. He was smiling and happy ; his receipts had amounted to 27,000 francs. What did the success of the performance and my state of mind matter to him !

My major-domo had accompanied me, and
very fortunately I found at the door my carriage,
which had arrived too soon, for fear that the
enthusiastic crowd would prevent me approaching it. Oh ! that enthusiastic crowd. I had
scarcely time to reach my hotel. Ten minutes
after the crowd was clamouring at the doors.
Shouts and vociferations filled the street. The
impresario knocked at my door, and sobbed some
articulate words, in which the words " magnificent
receipts—money lost," came as a thunderclap of
disaster. I had given him instructions to return
the money, but I felt that he would prefer to
give up his soul. Stones were thrown at my
windows, and I went to sleep lulled by the cries
of all the animals in creation.

We departed the following morning at nine
o'clock. What was my astonishment to perceive
on rising a crowd surrounding my carriage in
the street. A great part of the crowd had remained
there all the time, and it was amidst loud shouts
that my carriage set off, escorted by the army.
There was a detachment of soldiers at the station.
I saw the *impresario* arrive ; he was so yellow
that I understood at once that he had returned
the money.

Twenty-five years passed without my wishing
to return to Milan. Then one day I received a

deputation of young people from the town, bearing an address signed by more than 5,000 names.

I consented to go to Milan on condition that I should give *Phèdre* as the first performance. I determined that amends should be made to French poetry.

Phèdre met with a triumphant reception, and the curtain had to be raised twenty-two times after the performance. We were radiant with joy. But all the same, Italians do not like our French verse.

Vienna is one of the soils that have been most fertilized by our literature. There they adore French plays. This predilection is due to the initiative of a charming princess who loved France as a second country. I speak of the Princess de Metternich, who was, before the war of 1870, the idol of Parisians, and who continued for long years, and especially after the war, to hold the French flag in her aristocratic hands.

Thanks to her, for many years Vienna remained an open city for our literature, and a splendid field of combat where our dramatic works and our artists were always triumphant. Then the German influence commenced to undermine our influence, and eventually established its preponderance and that of the German spirit.

For a long time after 1870 I had refused to

play in Germany, in spite of all the proposals that were made me. Our misfortunes still throbbed in my heart, and I had had a violent altercation with the German Ambassador in Denmark. At a banquet which had been given for me by the King of Denmark, the Ambassador was placed near me. He was a charming man who was fond of the arts, but he was wanting in tact. I replied to the toast in my honour by a few happy words, when in a burst of enthusiasm my German neighbour tore the Prussian Eagle from his breast and tried to attach it to my dress.

My French blood boiled at this unwitting insult, and I crushed the Prussian Eagle under my feet. The incident was much spoken of and much written about in Germany, and all the pamphlets served as pennants to my name.

A few years ago, that is to say, more than six years before the war of 1914, a deputation from Alsace-Lorraine begged me to play at Strasbourg, Mulhouse, etc.

I consented immediately. But as soon as the performances were announced, it was forbidden to advertise them. And a personage from the German Government informed me that authority to play in Alsace-Lorraine would only be granted me, provided I would play, even if only once, in Berlin. Victorien Sardou happened to be present.

He discussed the matter in a lively manner with the representative of the German Government, who was, as a matter of fact, a courteous and cultivated man. I refused, however, to accept this condition. And it was not until two years later that I decided to play in Berlin. The committee of peace besought me in the name of the Alsace-Lorrainers. The address that was read to me was so touching that I accepted the invitation. The Berlin newspapers burst into a pæan of joy.

The announcement of my performances at the Schauspielhaus, the Imperial theatre of Berlin, started the excitement. All the seats were taken up, and two days after the announcement of the performances, not a vacant seat was left to the public. Seats bought and sold by speculators fetched exorbitant prices.

The spirit of hatred was unchained. An attaché to the French Embassy sent me a photograph he had taken showing the public which swarmed around the booking office, and the crowd which waited in and blocked the adjacent streets. Mounted police had been called in. It was very amusing to see. My arrival in Berlin had been signalled, and the crowd which thronged the quays and the streets was menacing but silent. At the hotel entrance the crowd was a little more cosmopolitan, and a little less barbarous. A young girl approached to hand me some flowers, but a brute snatched them out of her hands. A murmur of disapproval passed through the crowd. I kissed the child.

None present will ever forget the evening of this first performance. I had selected *Feodora*, a play that was then being acted by the idol of Berlin with great success. This choice was made deliberately. It was a battle that had to be fought. And I, who am so liable to stage fright, had no fear, for with me stage fright assumes a curious form ; in front of a public which I feel to be hostile for one reason or another I am free from all stage fright ; I have only one idea, one resolve : to subjugate the refractory audience. In front of a benevolent public, on the other hand, I am alarmed lest I should not come up to expectations, and stage fright grips me imperiously.

Now for this performance the contingent of police had been trebled. The authorities were nervous. I could see nothing but pale and strained faces. The artists, huddling in little groups, spoke in low tones, Mlle. Seylor, who played the little moujik, sobbed, and a moment before the curtain went up I heard some one saying to the *impresario* :

" She must not go on. We must go away.
A misfortune is going to happen."

At length the curtain was slowly raised, and
the poor moujik, shaken with sobs, went on the
stage and announced :

" The Princess Fedora ! "

The heaviness of the moment that precedes
the storm, and the rumbling of distant peals of
thunder alone can give you an idea of the
clamour of that crowd.

I entered the stage and remained for a second
nonplussed ; I was expecting a noisy and hostile
demonstration. A cold and dismal silence had
taken the place of the clamour. There was not
the least movement. The act proceeded with its
affecting incidents without the silence being disturbed. Then the curtain fell on the piercing
screams of the princess, maddened with grief, on
the corpse of her lover. A second passed. Then
a male voice exclaimed :

" Admirable ! "

And the storm that threatened broke out in
an unforeseen manner in thunderous applause.
The curtain was raised five times. The brilliant
and bejewelled public was on its feet, profoundly
moved, trembling, and enthusiastic. The evening continued in the manner it had begun.
Students cleared out the stock of a florist, and

covered the stage with flowers. Elevated by the love that I had just inspired, I felt that I had been touched by the wings of a god, and throughout the remainder of the play I multiplied my faculties of impersonation a hundredfold.

Outside a crowd of curious sightseers was waiting, kept in check by mounted police. I was standing up in a carriage bowing and returning thanks, when cries of " Vive la France ! Vive la France ! " stabbed me with such joy that in my turn I burst into sobs.

This cry, uttered by mouths that were only going to open for insults, this cry of " Vive la France," uttered by German throats, was one of the most touching triumphs of my career.

I gave a performance of *Phèdre* at the Opera, which was an uninterrupted series of ovations.

It must be recognized that the German public is never insensible to art or to profundity of thought. It is assuredly a public of a superior type from the standpoint of emotion.

I have often been to England. In my opinion the English people are the most hospitable in the world. Their hospitality is simple and generous. When he has opened his door, the Englishman never closes it. He pardons your faults and accepts your caprices. And it is thanks to this breadth of outlook that I have been beloved and spoilt for more than twenty-five years. Some evenings in London might be considered as the finest in my career. From my first visit with the Comédie Française, I have returned more than twenty times. The public have always received me in the warmest manner and showed themselves faithful, and even affectionate.

The American public is of a different type from the English public. It does everything on a large scale. Ah ! that landing of mine in America, the thousands of hands shaking mine until it was crushed. Those tyrannical reporters :

" What do you eat on waking up, Madame ? "

" Are you Jewess, Catholic, Protestant, Mohammedan, Buddhist, Atheist, Theist, or Deist ? "

And the Customs House ! an army of officers to investigate my forty-two boxes.

Finally there was the public, the real theatrical public. The performances that I gave at New York were acted to enthusiastic houses. I cannot quote a more perfect example of the admiring feelings of the crowd than by describing the last performance before my departure for Boston. When I arrived at the theatre, on Saturday, the 4th December, for a *matinée*, my carriage was stopped about twenty yards from the entrance ; it could not get any nearer as the street was

L

crowded with ladies sitting down, some on chairs borrowed from neighbouring shops, others on folding stools which they had brought themselves. I was twenty-five minutes getting to the stage-door. Hundreds of people shook my hand, begging me to return. One lady removed her brooch and fastened it to my mantle.

At each step I took I was detained. One lady had the idea of producing her pocket-book and asking me to write my name. The idea spread like lightning. Very young people made me write my name on their cuffs. I was completely exhausted. My arms were loaded with small bouquets. I felt some one behind me pulling my hat. I turned round quickly. A lady with a pair of scissors in her hand was trying to cut a lock of my hair ; but she only succeeded in cutting my feather. Detectives had to be fetched to liberate me, which they did without any ceremony. These policemen were real brutes.

I played *La Dame aux Camélias*, and I counted seventeen calls after the third act and twenty-nine after the fifth. In consequence of the cheering and the calls, the play lasted an hour longer than usual.

I was just about to leave when my *impresario* Jarrett came to tell me that there were more than 50,000 people waiting outside. Thanks to a ruse (my sister put on my clothes) I succeeded in escaping from this despotic enthusiasm. My sister was taken for myself, which enabled me to enter my carriage unperceived ; she returned to the hotel an hour after me, worn out with fatigue, but very amused at her " success."

I also visited Boston, where the ladies are in the majority. With the Bostonians I spent two charming weeks, my mind being on the alert all the time. The Boston women are puritans, but indulgent and without bitterness. Chaste and reserved, the resources of their hearts are expended on intellectual things : they are extremely fond of music, the theatre, literature, painting, and poetry. The performances that I gave at Boston were played before considerable audiences ; the seats had been put up for auction and had fetched high prices.

At Montreal I was also awaited by a public full of enthusiasm, which possessed a peculiar charm of youth and animation which impressed me. They let down on to the stage baskets of flowers and doves, from a pulley fixed to the roof of the house. Various songs were sung in my honour, including the Marseillaise.

The Bishop of Montreal had thundered against me, spreading calumnious attacks on my comrades and myself, as well as French art. As a reply to these insulting tirades, the admirers of France and of French art unyoked my horses, and my sleigh was almost carried by an immense crowd, amongst whom were the deputies and notabilities of the city.

All the other American towns that I visited, large or small, received me in the same manner.

A bishop or a clergyman would accuse us of leading souls to perdition, and then the crowd would become more numerous and admiring in proportion to the severity of the sermon.

Many a time I felt incensed at the indiscretions of advertisement, and could scarcely keep myself from abusing the stupid reporters. How many sandwich boards I should have liked to smash. I was not made for this excessive publicity with formidable accessories. I could not get used to it. And yet I was represented as the instigator of all the noise that went on around me. I was followed by my portion of inevitable calumnies. I would forget them, and only remember the spontaneous affection of the public of all the countries I have visited, who hailed me as the mouthpiece of the limpid and charming poetry of the genius of France.

Miscellaneous Hints

I HAVE talked a great deal about myself, my taste for poetry, for certain dramatic characters, and the reasons which have impelled me to hold in high esteem certain male parts for which I consider a feminine interpretation to be necessary. If I have also referred to the different receptions I have met with from the most various types of public, it has not been in order to mention my success and to dilate upon this subject. My aim has been to show that in resolving to win the affection of those who are attracted to art and the ideal of beauty, one gains the attachment, stirs the pulse, and invades the thoughts of the best-informed public of whatever country it may be.

In this respect also I believe that woman has many advantages over man ; she overcomes resistance more easily, whether it be sulky or spiteful ; she melts the most solid ice of ill humour and of prejudice.

Moreover, I repeat that in our art woman may most easily triumph. And this is readily understood, for the desire to please, the solicitude to paint one's face and hide one's real feelings are qualities and defects that naturally belong more to woman than to man. Again, the grace of her body and the guile of her character render woman a being ten times more perfectible than man.

Go among the lower classes and take a young man and a young girl. Give these two persons the refined education that pertains to their sex, the education in worldly elegance, and you will make of the young man a clumsy blockhead, and of the girl an exquisite young lady who is able to show herself everywhere without astonishing anybody.

Woman assimilates either supercilious or plaintive graces, distinction, *comme il faut*, or breeding with a surprising facility.

I knew an actress, the daughter of a theatre attendant, who passed as a perfect woman of distinction. The truth is that she was quite *comme il faut*, if not really distinguished.

Men, on the contrary, are very slow to acquire worldly assurance, and some never acquire it. In a few years one could make a delightful duchess out of a Parisian errand girl, but one could never make a duke out of a street urchin or a bourgeois.

Another cause of the inferiority of men in our

art is the necessity of entering the theatre when very young. At fifteen a young girl has finished her studies, unless she intends to take a degree ; while a youth does not finish his until he is nearly eighteen. A young girl of fifteen is bright enough to be initiated into the facts of life without actually experiencing them, but a youth is timid, awkward, and brutal.

A man cannot acquire the air of a man of the theatre until after the age of twenty or twenty-two. Before this age he resembles a puppy whose paws are too big and clumsy. It is the same with his voice, which is late and slow in maturing, while a young girl has her voice ready at fifteen.

Moreover, the career of the actor is shorter than that of the actress.

I have often been asked how many hours I work a day. As a matter of fact, I have never actually learnt a part. I learn the structure of the part, and that by heart, word for word ; I mumble, I repeat the sentences so as to become absolute mistress of them in the rapidity of the dialogue, but once I know my lines perfectly, I do not bother about them any more.

Whatever I have to impart in the way of anguish, passion, or of joy, comes to me during rehearsal in the very action of the play.

There is no need to cast about for an attitude,

or a cry, or anything else. You must be able to find everything you want on the stage in the excitement created by the general collaboration. Actors who stand in front of a mirror to strike an attitude or try to fall down on the carpet of their room are fools. They will effect nothing at all this way.

Everything must come from suggestion. Each action of the actor on the stage should be the visible concomitant of his thoughts. To be sure there are various details with which he should be acquainted, such as his carriage, his walk, and his method of breathing, but he should not be conscious of these solicitudes on the stage ; they ought to disappear in the acting of the actor who is convinced that he is Hamlet or Theseus. He must think like these characters. The young actor will express himself through the force of his will.

There is one matter that does not receive sufficient attention in our elocution classes, and that is action. I fancy that many of our instructors have read Herault de Sechelles, and, like him, confuse action with declamation. I must protest against such an outrage on the truth.

Elocution is the art of saying, or of declaiming, beautiful verse or the splendid discourses of orators with the appropriate pathos or energy. But this has nothing to do with action, which may be all mimicry while remaining action. One may play a dramatic pantomime, like Jean Richepin's *Pierrot Assassin*, or an emotional drama like Michel Carre's *L'Enfant prodigue*, or a melodrama like *La Main*, but there is not a trace of elocution in these artistic exhibitions, where only action plays a part. And it is only action that arouses the emotion or the terror of the public. Elocution and action may be mutually exclusive. When they are combined, it is so much the better for the public, but the actor must never forget that action is the supreme mistress ; and this our pupils do not suspect.

They think about inflexion and effects, but never of action. This is not really their fault. The first care of an instructor should be to teach his pupil articulation, breathing, the art of reciting verse. Then when the pupil knows all this, he should be compelled to think. And it is through this " thinking " that he will slide into action.

It happened one evening at the Comédie Française, when I was playing *Gabrielle*, that I could not hit upon the four lines that I had to say concerning the influence of Spring. The prompter was fast asleep. I substituted for these four lines a dumb-show that was so frantic and so fetching that the whole house burst into two rounds of repeated applause.   On leaving the stage, Madeleine Brohan exclaimed :

" You know, Sarah, that it was much better like that ! "   (It is only fair to add that the lines were by Emile Augier.)

Hippolyte Clairon, who was a great actor of the year 1700, asserted that it was necessary to change the intonation of the voice each instant.   This is pure folly, and the worst advice to give to young actors.   One should not be concerned about his voice when engaged in any kind of action.   The necessary modulations will take place in the course of the dialogue or monologue, just as it would be useless to try to move this or that muscle of the face to express the various phases of thought, for the expression of the face will vary in the course of the soliloquy.   In fact, I go so far as to say that one should think of nothing after the curtain has been raised.   All that he has learnt and retained will come to the aid of the actor without his being aware of it ; and the series of rehearsals of a play will give sufficient practice to the arms and legs to enable the actor to move from left to right, to enter from the back-scene, from the side ; to sit on the sofa, on the table, on the ottoman, to stretch himself on a lounging chair, without being conscious of doing so.   Once the curtain is raised, the actor ceases to belong to himself, he belongs to his character, to his author, to his public. He must do the impossible to identify himself with the first, not to betray the second, and not to disappoint the third. And to this end the actor must forget his personality and throw aside his joys and sorrows. He must present the public with the reality of a being who for him is only a fiction. With his own eyes, he must shed the tears of the other. With his own voice, he must groan the anguish of the other. His own heart beats as if it would burst, for it is the other's heart that beats in his heart. And when he retires from a tragic or dramatic scene, if he has properly rendered his character, he must be panting and exhausted. The reader will say that the life of an actor will quickly be exhausted by this physical and moral fatigue renewed evening after evening, but this is an error, as anguish and laughter become gymnastic exercises of the lachrymose and risorial glands, which gradually respond to the calls made on them, just as the limbs of the body will exceed the normal strength of men through exercise. The real fatigue is not that of the body, but that of the mind, which makes a fearful expenditure of will power. The only way to avert this genuine danger is to recuperate one's shattered strength by sleep. An actor must be

able to sleep, to sleep a good deal, at least eight
hours a day.   Sleep is essential to the repose of
our mind, and not less necessary for our vocal
chords.   For the vocal chords are affected by all
our actions, walking, reading, digestion, bathing,
riding, swimming, breathing.   All sports are
injurious to the beauty of the voice, but the most
injurious of all is boating, which will destroy the
strongest voices.   I could enumerate ten of our
young actors whose voices have been broken
through their fondness for rowing.   It is said
that Demosthenes walked along the sea-shore with
stones in his mouth, and practised pronunciation
in this way to cure his unfortunate stuttering.   I
am disposed to think that if he succeeded in controlling his articulation, it was at the price of
breaking his voice, as the vocal chords will not
endure these sharp influxes of air.

The life of the actor is not always enviable, but
then what medal is without its reverse, what art is
without its vexations ?   But all these difficulties
are capable of being overcome gradually by
patience, faith, and intelligence.   The joys that
art dispenses with prodigality when all the
obstacles in the path have been overcome by per-
severing effort and the maintenance of constant
discipline, compensate a hundredfold the minor
joys which this discipline prohibits.   It is enough

to be launched on the chosen career, and, if this choice is properly made, to pursue it to the end. And here also a perspicuous mind will render the most useful services.

The Influence of the Theatre

THE status of the actor is very often decried and scorned. The public comes to the theatre, but pays little attention to its protagonists, although in the end it covers with a glory that is sometimes effulgent the best among them. Moralists, and particularly religious moralists, pillory actors in general, and regard the theatre as a place of perdition. Thus in the majority of American towns where I gave performances in the course of my tour, the bishops launched thunderbolts from their pulpits designed to reduce my comrades and me to cinders. In connection with a sermon of this kind, my manager, Mr. Henry Abbey, wrote the following letter to the Bishop of Chicago :

" YOUR GRACE, Whenever I visit your city, I am accustomed to spend four hundred dollars in advertising. But as you have done the advertising for me, I send you two hundred dollars for your poor. "HENRY ABBEY."

174

I will pass over the excessive Puritan fanaticism which only sees in the theatre an invitation to debauchery, and regards actors as individuals with dissolute manners. Nor will I pause to show how odious this conception is. I will merely demonstrate that the influence of the theatre is far from being injurious. On the contrary, it seems to me that this particularly living, poetic and stimulating art is not only a delicate and delightful pleasure, but a perennial and effective form of instruction.

Of course, the pleasure of this instruction is not experienced in the same way by all the spectators. The public is made up of heterogeneous elements: there are the intellectuals, the sceptics, the simple, the coarse, and the impersonal. But all of them derive a certain instruction from this pleasure.

As soon as the first performance of a work has started, the intellectuals take a delight in disentangling the idea of the author, and seeking the philosophical side of the play. They attempt to divine the state of mind of the characters that are developing in front of them. They outstrip the march of the play, and reach the denouement with the author. Yet sometimes the course of the play shifts, and then the intellectual is annoyed at a solution towards which his logic had not led him. The simple-minded believe that it has all happened, and although they may not savour the philosophy of the work, they feel the effects of its shocks, and resolve to avoid all conduct that would bring them to a similar situation. The coarse-minded see nothing but the brutal fact, do not ask themselves why, do not discern the reason, and do not reason out the conclusion. Just as the blow of the fist leaves a mark, so they will retain a recollection of the fact that has struck them, and derive from it whatever instruction their minds are capable of receiving. As to the impersonal members of the audience, the crowd, that hideous monster, that hydra with a thousand heads, two thousand arms, two thousand legs, its heart and mind are borrowed of him who leads it ; so much the better for it if the latter be noble, so much the worse if he be a brute. The crowd follows him, intelligent or stupid, ferocious or good-natured ; the crowd will only imbibe the instruc-tion indicated by its leader. But what does it matter, the crowd has numbers on its side—and although it is not important so far as the artistic value of the play is concerned, it is essentially cap-able of being influenced, and, whatever it may be, will receive the benefit of theatrical instruction.

It is a matter of considerable interest whether the play be a historical or philosophical drama. Witness the extreme pleasure that is derived from a play which stages these or those historical characters whose life incidents are familiar to every one. You see them developing, living, and thinking. It is no longer dry history, which only mentions the actions performed by the heroes ; their personality escapes you, as they are merely puppets whose actions seem barely intelligible or without interest. But let the dramatist enlighten you with the rays of psychology appropriate to each character, and without observing it, you will gradually become enthusiastic. And the instruction bears fruit : here you are becoming acquainted with the events and the springs of the events of a whole period of history, which formerly reposed in the dusty chambers of your memory.

Thus the theatre and dramatic art manifest themselves as the complement of history and of philosophy ; they develop the love of the good and the beautiful. Their devotees guard the sacred fire of art, art which in all its embodiments is the finest creation of the human mind. What would life be without art ? Science prolongs life. To consist of what—eating, drinking, and sleeping ? What is the good of living longer if it is only a matter of satisfying the requirements that sustain life ? All this is nothing without the charm of art. And of all the arts, that of the theatre is the most complete. It employs all the others. Just as each soul feels the need of prayer, so each mind needs to evoke dreams, to create legends, and to conjure up the departed. It is necessary to go back far into antiquity to discover the first traces of the theatre, and this evocation of the ideal is a need even among savage peoples. I have been present at a festival given in my honour by Iroquois Indians. There could be no better example of this evocation than their war-like dance, with its shouts, and bellowings, the laughter of the victors, the sobs and groans of the vanquished, mimic combats, and burials, the whole accompanied by a frightful, lugubrious, and strident music. All who were present with me at this savage festival had the vision of an encounter between Whites and Iroquois, in which of course the Whites were vanquished, massacred, tortured, and finally eaten. Well, that savage mimicry exerted such a power, there was such a force of hatred in the death dance of these wretched people, the recent past was so vividly evoked, there was such a gratification of ferocious malice in the expressions of this band that the pity with which they inspired me changed into an appreciation that was fairer and truer. For their hatred they had paid such a heavy price, and all that I knew about the terrible war waged against them, the extortions, the vexations, the oaths violated by their conquerors, all this rose up before me, and I was forced to admit their right to hate.

I, too, derived instruction from the exhibition, coarse though it was, of these unfortunate people. In all times the theatre has been a vehicle of instruction and even an arena for artistic revolutionary movements ; the theatre is the most direct speaking-trumpet of new philosophical, social, religious and moral ideas. This century, which seems to be the era of liberty, will doubtless bring us many surprises, and the theatre will give us our first intimation of them.

" The audience must not leave the theatre," said Victor Hugo, " without taking with it an austere and profound morality." This idea was that of all the idealists, with very few exceptions. It would seem that Jean-Jacques Rousseau did not like the theatre ; but Jean-Jacques was a philosopher who, after having cherished poetry and dramatic literature, belied himself later under the influence of the cold and methodical Diderot.

The theatre is a need of all nations, all peoples, and all individuals. All the young and vigorous peoples love the theatre. Witness young America, which adores the theatre and is adored by the theatre. All the famous artists, creative or interpretative, set sail towards this country of liberty, of beauty, and of life. It is true that old fogeys, bureaucrats, invalids, and the timorous accuse us of going there because of our fondness for dollars, and of coveting gold more than laurels. They are mistaken. Americans do not throw handfuls of gold at literary, musical, or dramatic stars ; but they love the theatre. They have all the youth, the warmth, and the strength of new blood ; they do not hesitate to run after a new emotion, and do not begin to weigh the *pros* and the *cons*. They go first, and criticize afterwards. They will return continually or never return again, according to whether they have been charmed or deceived.

These remarks do not apply to the Latin races, whose love of the theatre is less ardent, and much more superficial. Although all new ideas are born in France, they are not readily adopted there. It seems that they must first commence to prosper in a foreign country. The public do not like giving themselves the trouble to understand. Their attention is quickly fatigued. The new theatre of these latter years has perhaps abused the somewhat slender patience of our good-humoured public. Nevertheless, the function of the theatre consists precisely in inviting the public to think, to understand, and to extract from what happens on the stage something other than a vulgar pleasure of the eyes. Those who write for the theatre ought never to lose sight of this : they must contrive so that the crowd itself draws the profound and austere moral of which Victor Hugo speaks. Consequently, they must supply this crowd with the data whence a moral can be drawn, arranged in such a way that the conclusion may be inferred without hesitation or difficulty, and always with the adjuncts that are imperatively required by the theatre.

In recent years the theatre has not always been clear, instructive—or even theatrical. But it has been purified, and great figures and great works have emerged which respond to the requirements of the intellectual education of the masses. This production may be divided into three classes: realist drama ; realist-idealist drama ; and religious drama.

I have in mind particularly the works of Brieux for the realist-idealist theatre. These are powerful and suggestive plays.

Brieux has given us : *Les Bienfaiteurs, Blanchette, la Foi, la Robe Rouge, Maternité, les Remplaçantes*, etc. These bold, penetrating, and luminous plays are the masterpieces of realist drama. In them society is vigorously scourged, and the blemishes of social hypocrisy are laid bare. A magnificent conception of humanity is wrought out in these plays. And there is nothing in these philosophical, moral, or social doctrines that hinders the engrossing development of the plot.

It is all real drama, and Brieux is a splendid
apostle.

The apostleship of M. de Curel is less direct
and more intellectual. His work, however, is of
a peerless beauty. The drama *La Fille sauvage*
is to my way of thinking the masterpiece of a
mournful but grandiose philosophy. And I have
always been distressed because this work has not
found popular favour.

It is said that M. de Curel is indifferent to this
favour. I think he is wrong. The theatre has
a precise technique. And it is a great pity that a
man like Curel should neglect to acquire it. He
behaves like a preacher who would select a chapel
instead of a church, and would preach in Latin to
persuade, educate, and win his flock.

There is a fine dramatic sweep in the work of
Curel ; but it is broken by philosophical reason-
ing. Explanatory dialogues and dissertations
impede the action, and the fatigued public with-
draws its attention and loses interest. The work
does not catch on. And the instruction which it
contains is lost to thousands of persons.

The ease with which the theatre is able to influence the public, either through the sentimental
feelings aroused by the plot or through the more
or less subtle discourses spoken by the characters
of the play, has disquieted certain morose indi-

viduals, although most unreasonably so. For similar reasons many people will not allow young girls to go to the theatre, although they are much less severe in the case of the Opera or Comic Opera.

Once I expressed surprise to a charming lady of the faubourg Saint-Germain at the fact that young ladies never went to the performances of *La Dame aux Camélias*.

" Oh ! " she exclaimed, " my daughter knows the play."

" How's that, Madame ? Has she read it ? "

" Oh, no ! " rejoined the lady, a little shocked, " she has heard the opera *La Traviata*."

" But it seems to me," I answered, " that it is all the same."

" Oh no," said the lady.   " The music corrects the realism of the play.   My daughter did not pay any attention to the words of the music that she heard."

I was astounded at such an answer, and turned my back on the lady.

I have frequently heard the opinion expressed that religious subjects ought not to be put on the stage.   What a curious idea ! Happily broad-minded people are not influenced by these timorous souls.   The theatre is the involuntary reflex of the ideas of the crowd.   It progresses continually towards the conquest of the beautiful; sometimes it goes too quickly, it has hoped too much from the hearts and minds of the people ; the hour not having come, it is found necessary to retreat. This was the position of the religious question in the theatre twenty years ago. Many efforts in this direction had been made in France, but the march of events was retarded by superior forces. We had to stand aside to let the wave pass. But let our friends take heart. Everything that has been done in the way of religious works for the last twenty years is full of beauty, grandeur, and reverence.

A few years ago Edmond Haraucourt came to me to read his *Passion*. I was seized with admiration.

" This must be acted," I exclaimed. " I want the public to see this work."

But what battles, what rebuffs, what puerile excuses, and what cowardly attacks awaited us. Even that year it proved impossible to act the play without alteration. The author and I saw it through. Now " Quand même " is my motto. I determined *quand même* to compel the public to share my admiration and enthusiasm for this work. There were incidents both comical and unnerving. In the end we arranged a reading during an interval at the Pasdeloup concerts at the Cirque d'Hiver.

The hall was packed, but a hostile spirit prevailed. Our enemies had gathered in order to put an immediate stop to such a scandal. Well-meaning friends came to implore me not to carry out my intention.

" You will not be allowed to go through with it," they said.

" I tell you we shall read Haraucourt's *Passion* to the last word."

And I started to read this work of reverence and of beauty in front of a frigid audience. The most beautiful lines were accompanied by malicious whisperings. Being a woman, I had the advantage of not being interrupted. But when it was the turn of the actor who had to read the lines ascribed to Jesus, there was an outburst of cat-calls, shouts, and roars. We continued undisturbed to exchange replies. Finally, during a momentary silence a joker shouted :

" Miousic, Miousic ! "

And the public, tired of yelling, burst into laughter, suddenly realizing that laughter causes greater discomfort to the artist than hissing. For a moment I thought the cause was lost, when Edmond Haraucourt jumped up from his seat and turned on the audience, his face white with anger, and his teeth clenched.

" You came here knowing that a play in verse

entitled *La Passion* would be read. You have
paid for your seats, you will hear the play, or you
will depart."

And kissing my hand :

" Thanks, Madame, thanks ! "

The effect was withering ; the public, curbed
by this logic and intimidated by this faith, became
silent and listened without any demonstration.
The ice had been broken, and this daring attempt
caused great discussion. People argued against
this new tendency, but the work was splendid and
powerful, and was suffused with grandeur and
reverence. Victory rested with the vanquished.

Three years later, *La Passion* was performed in
a theatre, with scenery, lay figures, and costumes.
At the same time Edmond Rostand's *La Samaritaine*, a gospel in verse in three tableaux, was
triumphantly and gloriously launched. The day
of the first performance of *La Samaritaine* was a
day of unforgettable emotion. Christian love
filled the theatre with a joy of infinite purity. I
felt myself transported to the beyond as I recited
the beautiful words, and other hearts beat in my
heart as I wept those saltless tears devoid of
bitterness, those pure tears that lave, remove, and
wash away for ever the dross of our souls, of our
lives too long for the wrong that we do, too short
for the good that we could do. The audience

was transported and irradiated, and applauded all the lines. Catulle Mendès stood up and uttered cries of enthusiasm. This day was especially memorable for me, as it plunged me for a moment into memories of my early infancy, when, mystical and ignorant, I raved about the little Jesus ; it demonstrated to me more than ever the powerful influence of literary works performed in our temple : the Theatre.

On the following days I received numerous letters, and I quote a passage from one of them, written by a priest :

"MADAME,—I was present the day before yesterday at your performance of *La Samaritaine*. I will not conceal from you, Madame, the fact that I went there in a very bad humour. I wanted to hear the work which had not yet appeared in book form, as I was anxious to write a vigorous attack upon M. Rostand, for I deplored this attempt to enthrone religion in the theatre. I returned completely converted by your propaganda, Madame, for sitting by my side was a poor man with a tortured soul. During the performance he could not refrain from speaking to me and confiding to me his doubts and indecisions, and at length he exclaimed with a joyful and transfigured face that he felt better and restored. I am happy, Madame, that all that remains of my aggressive suspicions against you and M. Rostand is a touching and grateful recollection."

These few lines made me very happy, and my mind was at perfect rest during all the performances of *La Samaritaine*. It was God Himself who inspired the work of M. Rostand. This work resembles Samothrace's Victory, which bears in its outspread wings and fluttering tunic the immortal cry of glory of the ages that are past to the ages that are to come.

Our Art

ITS temple is the universe, with its seas, its mountains, its forests, its cities, its country-sides, and its rivers ; its blue or gray skies, its stars, and its planets.

Its orchestra is the howling blast and the gentle zephyr of the four winds, the reverberations of thunder, the swish of waves over the shingle, the roaring of wild beasts, the trill of birds, the love-song of lovers, the death-rattle of the dying, the wailing of human beings, the prayer of the faithful, the hearty laughter of the happy, the merry laughter of the innocent.

Its ideal is to achieve glory.

Its glory is to realize its ideal.

Our art is the finest, the noblest, the most suggestive, for it is the synthesis of all the arts. Sculpture, painting, literature, elocution, archi-tecture, and music are its natural tools. But while it needs all these artistic manifestations in order to be its whole self, it asks of its priest or priestess one indispensable virtue : " faith."

189

By means of faith an actor who is badly endowed by nature will captivate a prejudiced audience.

Faith will enable an artist to impose upon the public a fresh incarnation of a character already created by an actor of genius, which character, adopted by successive generations, has become " the tradition."

The Tradition ! That which must not be touched ! Horrible and stupid tradition ! The axe with which they try to cut the sprouting wings of neophytes.

" Tradition," such a solemn word, and uttered by such solemn voices ! a word that freezes budding personalities ! Nothing is more remote from truth than tradition. Nothing is more injurious to the ripening of thought.

There cannot be any real tradition ; for it is impossible that a fair and well-bred person should speak and behave like a dark and vulgar person. And yet both might find themselves in an identical situation, either dramatic or comic, in which they would be obliged to repeat the same words ; but these words, albeit the same, would form graceful or vulgar sentences. These sentences would be uttered by a melodious or by a broken voice, expressed by a comely or a ravaged face, accompanied by a graceful or an awkward gesture.

Well then, without carrying to extremes (as I

am doing) the distance between the creator of a
part which sets a tradition, and the new artist
who desires to interpret the character already
created, there is a distinction, even if it only
resides in the mind, and the mind being our
superior agent, this fact alone renders it impossible
for us to manifest a traditional style.

Moreover, it is extremely rare that artists
inspired by faith will accept a tradition.

It is true that the dramatic art has passed
through the most various transitions. In the
time of the Greeks and Romans the actor himself counted for nothing. Whether he was handsome or ugly, elegant or ordinary, mattered not
at all ; he was the Herald of poesy ; he func-
tioned as a speaking trumpet.

Later on he was a poor wretch engaged in the
religious comedies which were enacted in the
churches, and which brought much money to the
cult.

They performed the Passion ; they were very
badly paid and roughly treated, but were allowed
to confess without charge. Then they were buffoons, the little Bohemian troup, invited by the
lords, hunted by the peasants, starving in the
ditches, hardened by the cold, or perishing of
thirst in the ditches dried up by the sun.

But nothing avails to discourage one who is

stage-struck, neither the affectionate and prudent remarks of mothers, nor the summary action of fathers, nor the coldness of esteemed relatives, nor the haughty aloofness of the imbecile and richly-clad plebeian, nor the first sarcasms, nor the checks, nothing, nothing !

Poverty leaves us frailer, paler, more like Hamlet.   It makes the voice hollow.

What matters poverty !   What matters anything to him who is " enamoured " of our art ! Does he not carry in himself every joy and every beauty ? . . .

His walls are of cardboard, and his mountains painted on canvas.   His skies have their nights illuminated by a thousand little paper stars suspended on the end of a thread and stirring with every puff of breath.

His impregnable turrets are fashioned of millboard, and the axe which is laid to them and the bullet which pierces them are children's toys. But the hand which holds these toys, is the hand of a man electrified by splendid verse.

The heart that rushes to the assault beats a charge as vigorous, as precipitate as if a real enemy were in question.   And for the public that is present, anxious, nervous, and transported, the turret might be of freestone, the sky the black firmament, lit by its thousands of golden studs. And it is the faith of the actor, holding the torch handed him by the poet, that illumines every mind, every soul, and every sensibility.

Faith is necessary to our art to such an extent that eventually it is identified with, and becomes part of, ourselves.

And here I recall a pretty incident, which I cannot refrain from mentioning.

In a little town near Lille two poor old artists were living in retirement, far from everything. They both made shift on their meagre pensions from the Société des Artistes dramatiques. A thousand francs perhaps between them. Were they married? Nobody could say. The woman, who had taken the parts of a *confidente* in tragedy, still retained a mask of beauty. The regular lines of her face imparted chastity to the whiteness of her braided hair. He was an old provincial comedian, with a grimacing and vivacious face.

They lived happily enough, it seemed, recalling the joys, the fears, the intoxications of former days.

On Christmas Eve, while they were strolling in the little garden that was their delight, two rascals broke into their tiny dwelling and carried off all their savings.

They regarded each other in blank despair on

discovering their misfortune. They resolved to
bear patiently the privations which this loss would
inflict on them until the 26th December, when
their little allowance would arrive ; for they were
aware that poor actors would not be able to obtain
a morsel of bread on credit in a place where they
had never owed a farthing.

On inspecting the larder, they discovered that
there remained a little veal, a tin of sardines,
some cheese, and some bread. The cellar, represented by an old box, contained a bottle of wine,
half full, and a bottle of beer. The aspect of
the cellar left them sad and desolate : not a
bundle of wood, not a small lump of coal. And
the weather was so cold. The wind howled
through the cracks in the doors and the broken
window panes.

The poor old people repaired to the little room
which adjoined the bedroom and was used as
a dining and sitting-room. Fire still glowed
through the gray ashes of coal. They brought
up their chairs quite close, without a word, their
sad looks fixed on the future. Before going to
bed, they covered up the dying fire with infinite
precautions.

The morning found them before the chimney-
piece. Thick flakes of snow were falling.

At the end of the day, the meagre repast con-

sumed, the poor old people crouched closer and
closer together. Their chairs touched, their
hands clasped, and their feet stretched towards
the lukewarm little fire.   And they talked about
the triumphs of other days.   They chattered of
this person, dead, of that person, disappeared.

"Do you remember," she said at length, "of
the burst of applause which greeted my entry
when I was about to announce to Cæsar that
Cleopatra wanted to see him, if it were only for a
moment?"

"Yes," he replied, drawing up closer to her,
"you were wearing a gold-braided petticoat and
a green scarf."

They drew even closer together, he, pale and
rigid with the cold, saying :

"You tell me that the fire is warming.   I do
not feel it, but I believe it is so."

And they chatted away until morning, making
merry over the recital of their old adventures,
quavering Christmas carols, laughing softly ;
finally happy to be still alive when so many others
had disappeared, and to have still a little warmth,
when so many others were cold.

When daylight penetrated into the room, they
perceived that the fire was out, and had no doubt
been so for a long time ; but the gold spangles
off the Egyptian petticoat had fastened on to the

blackened cinders, and had warmed them like a theatre fire, by the suggestion of " faith."

We must not, however, confuse " faith " with bumptiousness ; for in our art there is, alas, a host of actors and actresses, with very comical appellations—haven't you seen them ?—who have no doubts about anything.   They are like moths who break their feelers against a closed window, or scorch their wings in the flame of a candle. But these I leave on one side.   They have no conception of the beauty of our art, nor of the mission of its apostles.   In the theatrical career, as in other careers, there are misfits and failures who take up too much room, speak too loudly, stand bravely before crowds, pose as unappreciated geniuses, and fall victims to absinthe.   The public too often confuses them with true artists. But what does it matter ?   We artists follow our path, so arduous, so full of snares, but so bedecked with flowers.

It is our mission to stimulate the minds and move the hearts of men.   The poets and dramatists entrust us with the finest products of their art.   They place in our trembling but confident hands the quintessence of their minds, the flesh of their flesh, their long-meditated utterances, the generous thoughts they would sow in the heart of crowds, the lesson they would teach society in an entertaining manner, without direct affront to the listener. And under the mask of laughter, they extract from a ludicrous situation a new injunction against this or that abuse.

And we are the advocates in these proceedings. We alone may communicate instantaneously to the public the ardent faith of the author.

It is we who must, with one hand, snatch away the tares, and with the other sow the good seed.

Ah ! What intense joy steals over the actor when he feels that a trembling audience is hanging on his lips and his looks, while he knows that behind the scenes is a person whose heart is beating quickly, who has taken two years of his life to elaborate what often proves to be a masterpiece ; who has erased, corrected, rejected words, sentences, and lines ; who has so much at stake, his future, sometimes even his daily bread, his glory, his all.

And in the drama which is enacted there, where all the author's future is involved, it is not he who holds the dice ; he has placed everything into the frail hands of women, into the rough hands of men. Oh ! we feel this heart that beats behind us even in our hearts, we hear it in our ears, and when at length the audience crowns the play with its approval, we experience the infinite enjoyment of the martyr at the extremity of his suffering, or of the lover in the realization of his dream.

This sensation is denied the author. But it is so fugitive that he has no need to envy us. In fact, his work, which we have launched, soars higher and higher into the infinity of time.

But when our work is over, the glory does not survive our lives, and often expires before us. How many illustrious actors have I seen draping themselves in the folds of a dead glory, affecting and grotesque in their resolve to live once more when their course was run ! But our mission is fine enough, and our art sufficiently copious. We have nothing of which to complain. When I was young I resented the infamous libels thrown at our art. Now I regard those who do not know or do not want to know without anger, but with profound pity. What then does it matter to me that people think or do not think this or that ? In life we love a select number of beings, who are our universe. In art, we work for a select number of minds, who are our judges, our supreme arbiters. And I would ask this question : when one dies, for whom does one die ? The actor must never work for the crowd, for nothing is easier than to win popular applause. He must never rest satisfied, even if success crowns his efforts, for he has always something to learn, even when he seems to be perfect.

I have a great contempt for the art of those actors who, having established a vogue, never alter their pose, or their inflexions, or their expressions. They are admired by some. For my part I deny that they have individualities. They are merely good workmen, who have laboured diligently and repeat an identical performance, alike at each day and each hour. It is not art ; it is following a trade. But the public often confuses the one with the other.

How many actors and actresses have I heard boast without any other justification than a good memory for those rehearsals during which they have been coached in their lines and their inflexions, with an indication of the pose, the time, the rhythm of the verse, the end of the sentence, and finally the place where they have to make the " effect ". For there are actors who look to nothing but the effect, that is to say, the applause of the crowd. And most often it is the *claque*, the odious *claque*, which gives the signal to the intense and overflowing delight of the public. The *claque* is an appropriate name, for it is a veritable slap in the face of Art and of the artist, who ought to give the signal for spontaneous applause —as Sardou says.

Well, then, I repudiate this strained and mechanical art.

Art is the expression of the manifold sentiments poured out by the author in the current of his work. You must weep real tears, suffer real anguish, laugh a real laugh which is contagious. You cannot really die every evening, you tell me? This is true enough. But birth and death are incidents which only happen once in the life of each human being, while joy and sorrow are recurring episodes in the existence of each and all.

Diderot contended that the artist ought not to feel anything.

This is an error and I declare Diderot to be wrong. This contention may have been justified in the time of the Greeks, when actors played in theatres holding twenty or thirty thousand spectators, when they donned masks, raised themselves by six inches, when they lengthened their arms by gauntlets which gave their limbs the proportions required by æsthetic beauty, when they raised their voices beyond all reason in order to be heard, and when delivery was cultivated solely with a view to rhythm. The actors of this age could not therefore import any personal emotion into their parts. They were, as I have said before, the speaking trumpets of the poet.

It devolved upon the chorus to express the different sentiments that animated the characters. Consequently, the tragedian was a living and talking puppet, nothing more. The chorus was his visible soul so far as the public was concerned.

These choruses were invested with such importance, especially in the tragedies of Æschylus, that when, after a performance of Eumenides, the chorus of Furies had inflicted a terrible fright upon the public, the magistrates passed a law limiting the number of members of a chorus to fifteen for tragedy and twenty-four for comedy.

But the understanding of the function of the theatre at which we have now arrived does not allow us to exclude personal sentiments and emotions. We must make our characters live. And in no way can we do this better than by quitting our own personality to enter that of another being.

Many times have I arrived at the theatre tired, suffering, and dejected ; then gradually I have entered into the life of the character I was personating. And in arranging my face I have changed it to a trifling extent, perceptible to myself, but almost invisible to the public. The character I had to personate being a violent and unfortunate woman, I would draw my eyebrows slightly together, and thicken them towards the middle. I would efface the bow of my upper lip to make it straight and implacable. And a mysterious coldness would then steal over my face. If, on the other hand, my character, as in the Queen of Ruy Blas, was a poor victim seeking the wherefore of life, I would efface my own eyebrows with white powder, and trace over them an interrogative and unquiet eyebrow, resembling that of Pierrot; I would shorten the corners of my mouth, and make the lower lip pout. This done, my face would amuse me by its devout naïveté.

And gradually I would become identified with my character; I would dress with care; I would dismiss Sarah Bernhardt to a corner, and leave her to be a spectator of my new " me." I would then enter the stage, ready to suffer, to weep, to laugh, to love, ignoring what my real " me " was doing downstairs in my dressing-room.

I remember that one day when I was playing Posthumia, an old blind woman of eighty, in *Rome vaincue*, five minutes before going on the stage I was gripped with such agony that I rolled about the corridor sobbing. M. Perrin, the manager of the Comédie Française, Georges Clairin the painter, and Paul de Remusat, who were present, sent for a doctor in a great fright. Suddenly during an abatement of the pain I heard the line that gave me my cue. I leapt up. I adjusted my white wig. And before the three of them had recovered from their surprise, I had parted the curtain of the Hall of Judgment. My face racked by suffering, my forehead knit by the will to suffer no longer, all my being trembling under the sting of the agonies I had just cast out of me, made such an impression upon the public, that they stamped with enthusiasm on my appearance.

I said my lines. I screamed my prayer. My shrivelled hands sought for the support that my blind eyes could not see. I left the stage sustained by the applause of the audience, but on the threshold of my dressing-room, the pains returned, and gripped me so violently that I lost consciousness.

Well, it is my firm conviction that all actors and actresses should not only transform themselves, but split their personalities in halves each day. They must forget their personal worries, their vexations, and their sufferings, in order to assimilate the worries and the vexations of the character they are to personate. And actors who cannot do this need not delude themselves ; they will never be able to carry away an audience.

The actor must give up his heart, his flesh, and his blood to that impersonal and capricious crowd, which always resists at first, and afterwards surrenders with a grace and indulgence that are unbounded.

Ah ! all these people who are attentively seated are really waiting to see the " tamer " devoured. And every public of every country is the same, when it is confronted by a dominating personality.

From the commencement of his career, the actor must resolve to be "somebody". But do not let neophytes be led astray. Nothing is more difficult than to retain this attribute of being " somebody ".

In our art, fame can be won in an hour ; but most often it is only the infatuation of an audience for an original posture, an unfamiliar head-dress, a daring gesture, or the vendetta of a coterie against one actor in favour of another. How culpable, stupid, and wicked are those who awaken the boundless pride of the upstart in the breasts of poor young actors, and for nothing at all ! In the course of my long career how many of these mediocrities have I seen raised upon the shield of glory by fools who cannot walk ten paces without tiring of shouting without echo, and who callously let fall the chosen one to break his back.

Permanent success cannot be achieved except by incessant intellectual labour, always inspired by the ideal.

And be it said that this ideal need not always be the same. Certainly not. It is the right, and even the duty of the ideal to change, as the constant evolution of society, of politics, of manners, and even of customs does not permit of an immutable ideal.

But whatever may be the play that is performed, of whatever type may be the action, wherever the place may be where the incidents happen, there is always an ideal, towards which the chief efforts of the actor should be directed. To create a character, however contemptible it might be, the actor must seek for the flame that illumines it.

The great mistake which the majority of actors commit is that in the first vision evoked by the reading of a play, they already see the character that is entrusted to them dressed, walking, and living. It is not one artist who has confessed this fact to me, but thirty or forty actors and actresses.

This fault is so serious that it is sometimes difficult to remedy it. An actor hearing an author read a play in which he is to impersonate a character ought never to be told in advance the part which is to be assigned to him, as otherwise he only pays a languid attention to everything that is not his part, and the ideas of the author escape him. He forgets too often that he is not himself the keyboard, but that he forms part of a general harmony.

To create a character with success, the actor must become his friend every hour, and his shadow every minute. The actor must give the character a soul, a heart, lungs, a brain, arms, legs. The soul may be disturbed or limpid ; the heart may palpitate or beat calmly ; the lungs may breathe healthily or rattle ; the mind may be simple, imposing, or cunning ; the arms may be graceful, powerful, or drooping ; the legs may walk with dignity, shamble with nonchalance, or strike the heel with pride. For everything must play a part in the creation of a character : the poise of the head, the authority of the gesture, the manner of sitting, of rising, of coming in, of going out. All this is necessary to evoke in the public mind the living personification of the author's dream. Afterwards come the head-dress, the costume, and the touching-up of the face.

It is often difficult to cast off one's own material personality.

It is then necessary to add something, and not to suppress. For example, nothing short of dumbness would have disguised that voice of Coquelin's which was so well known to thousands.

Salvini, however great his genius, would never

have been able to play a dwarf, by reason of his colossal stature. It would have been impossible for that delightful artist Rejane to play Ophelia, for Mounet Sully to interpret Figaro ; for me to play the nurse in *Les Remplaçantes* by Brieux.

But, excepting a few rare cases, actors should attempt to interpret every type of character. It is bad policy to stick to one line of business. A young man with an attractive person should be able, if he is usually the Lover, to play when he likes a comic character, an old man, a peasant.

A tragedian should play modern comedy very frequently, even if his efforts in this direction are not so happy. He will find that his inflexions gain in variety. He will check the tendency to excessive solemnity which comes from the interpretation of classic tragedies.

The *tragédienne* will benefit from acting in modern plays. Those *tragédiennes* who only play tragedy have a heavy step, slow and pensive elocution, and solemn gestures.

The same observation applies to the comic actor. He should embark without hesitation, not upon tragedy if his nose forbids this step, but upon the pathetic drama. It is meet that he who shakes the body with laughter should sometimes moisten the eye with tears.

But France, the home of the arts and of liberal

ideas, is also the country of a superabundant
bourgeoisie. And the bourgeois classifies and
isolates everything, as he himself is voluntarily
classified and isolated in the narrow shell of the
bourgeois. He likes particular painters to exe-
cute particular types of pictures, and insists that
these pictures should be of a specific size. He
will not allow a sculptor to be a painter, or a
painter a musician, or a musician an architect,
or an author an actor, or an actor a writer. He
would never have allowed Æschylus, Euripides,
Molière, or Shakespeare to be actors as well as
poets ; Aristodemus to be an ambassador as well
as an actor ; Leonardo da Vinci and Michelangelo to be politicians, painters, and sculptors.
He still laughs at the violin of Ingres, and now
that he is in the majority, he imposes his will
upon actors.

There is the lover, the *jeune premier*, the comic
character, the noble father, the third part, the
tragedian, the confidant. There are equivalent
types of actresses, to which may be added the
coquette and the artless maiden.

It is impossible to condemn too severely this
state of affairs ; for the habit of playing a single
line of business relieves the gifted and intelligent actor from the necessity of perfecting himself. He is satisfied the moment he imperson-

ates the character he is accustomed to represent.

The Conservatoire manufactures types of marionettes. And it is a great misfortune that no desire exists to remodel its method of instruction from top to bottom.

But this Conservatoire, which is necessary and indeed indispensable, is steeped in the bourgeois spirit.

I appreciate the fact that our Ministers have more important matters to attend to. Yet the state of the theatre should not leave them wholly indifferent ; for it is the spring-board of all the intellectual conflicts which often terminate in revolutionary struggles.

It is an immense bow from which the genius of poets shoot malignant and beneficent arrows into society and the moral code.

It has served as a pulpit for preaching the greatest causes and the noblest aspirations.

The theatre propagates new ideas, it arouses slumbering patriotism, it exposes turpitudes and abuses by sarcasm, educates the ignorant without their knowing it, stimulates those of little courage, strengthens faith, gives hope, and enjoins charity.

The rôle of the actor, so often decried, is not insignificant in the light of this apostleship. It is all the more necessary that he, whose voice is

to give utterance to the message of poets and
dramatists, should be provided by an up-to-date
system of instruction with the means of making
himself perfectly understood.

APPENDIX

Hints for Making-up

MAKING-UP is one of the greatest difficulties that confront a beginner, who has many pitfalls to avoid in this department. How the actor looks from the auditorium is an important factor in his success. A face that is very pretty at home or at a party may be insipid and commonplace on the stage, and quite insignificant. It may even become ridiculous under the influence of the footlights, which change the form of the shadows of the face and almost completely transform the details of the features as well as the physiognomy as a whole. The actor must therefore see himself as he looks in the theatre, and rectify as a sculptor would whatever imperfections his face may contain. If his features are naturally strong and marked, the nose too prominent, the forehead protruding, the cheekbones projecting, or the chin too square, he must soften them gently, without however flattening them. They must be shaded off.

On the other hand, rouge on the cheeks, pencilling round the eyes, and the darkening of the eye itself can work a transformation in a featureless face, giving it the accentuation desired.

An insipid face with small eyes is especially to be dreaded. It may be mitigated by an enlargement of the eyes effected by means of a blue or chestnut-coloured pencil which stretches the eyelids. The make-up of the eyes and mouth changes the entire pattern of a face. The care with which this is done should therefore outweigh the make-up of every other part of the face : cheeks, ear lobes, nose, etc.

Knowledge of this art can hardly be acquired except from experience, and I would add personal experience. Each face requires special treatment, and its owner can only learn to utilize what is most suitable to it after many experiments.

There are, however, some general principles that should apply to everybody, and it is the duty of those who practise them to impart their knowledge to neophytes.

Making-up is not the same thing for men as for women. It may be more elaborate in the case of women, who must aim at correlating the face of the actress with one of the types of perfect feminine beauty, the woman's part much more than the man's part being to delight the eye.

But women cannot all make-up according to the same rules. A brunette may not treat her face in the same way as a blonde.

A dark actress should use ochre or saffron powder for the complexion and very little rouge on the cheeks ; on the other hand, she should apply plenty of rouge to the ears, and take care to hide the slight down which a woman of thirty has around the lips. This down, which is pleasant to look upon at close quarters, assumes a dirty aspect behind the footlights, which disfigures the prettiest face. A little white grease dabbed above the upper lip and at the corners of the lips will repair the defect.

A dark woman should always expose a part of her forehead, in order to lighten her face. She should not put black around the eyes, but only lengthen the eye with a chestnut-coloured pencil, never a black pencil. She may rouge the lips as much as possible, especially if she has white teeth. But rouge grease must not be used, as it weakens articulation. Liquid rouge, containing a very little vinegar, or varnish, or acetate, must be employed. One need not fear that this will dry up the lips in the daytime. I can give an assurance that this will not do any harm, or detract from the beauty of a pretty mouth. This mixture has the advantage of remaining unaffected by the saliva ; it imparts to the lips a flexibility that enables them to open and shut, thus doubling the emphasis of a word.

The basic complexion is not so dark in the case of blondes as in the case of brunettes. Rouge should be employed more lavishly, and it should be more vivid, and less yellow. The powder that softens the whole may be either " natural " or " Rachel ". The eyelids should be made either clear chestnut-colour, or blue, for preference, which emphasizes the blue of the pupils. Rouge applied to the corner of the eye enlarges it. Rouge should be applied high up on the cheeks, while the mouths of blondes should be clearer, of a fairly vivid rose rouge.

Both brunettes and blondes should lengthen the eyelashes which shade the glance with some " Rimmel ". If they are anxious that the elongation should be more pronounced, they should use some cosmetic, which has the advantage of not making the eyes smart and water. Rouge should be applied inside the nostrils.

In a general way make-up should be related to the dimensions of the theatre. The larger the house, the heavier the " make-up ". And this is understandable. The actor's features are diminished by distance so that spectators scarcely perceive them.

Their importance must be restored. The same remark applies to the subject of the intensity of light that darkens the reliefs.

The more powerful and diffused the light is, the more the reliefs may be accentuated. Very little acquired skill is sufficient to modify, accentuate, or diminish without artificial agency. For instance a nose that is too long or too large may be diminished and rendered elegant if one takes the precaution to smear the rouge over the nose as well as the cheeks, leaving untouched the mesial line that is naturally clear.

The mouth is susceptible of complete transformation. It may be entirely suppressed by means of white grease, or shaped according to inclination by means of rouge. A large mouth with thin lips becomes a mouth with cherry lips, and lips that are too full are made thinner and longer. The eye and even the white of the eye are enlarged. I knew an actress who had little eyes, but the arch of her eyebrow was so lofty and so marked that it permitted the delineation of artificial eyes in blue. And to the audience she appeared to have fine large eyes.

These arrangements and these adjustments are not solely designed to neutralize natural imperfections, or to counteract the amplitude of the stage and of the auditorium, or the intensity of light, but are also intended to meet the requirements of the part to be interpreted. The build of the actor or actress does not always correspond perfectly with that of the character they are impersonating. A slight retouching, delicate and pru-

dent, is not out of place. It is very necessary to be
familiar with the psychology of the character and the
ideas of the author. The occasion then demands an
expert and tactful hand to lengthen and soften the eye,
or harden it and set it in dark circles ; to shorten the
mouth and give it a delightful pout, or give it an implacable
cleavage.

The same necessities may lead to a total transformation of the physiognomy and a drastic modification of
every feature. A young girl may appear as an old
woman of eighty. An actress of more than ripe age
often manages to pass for a young lady in love. But
these complete transformations are more appropriate to
the devices of masculine make-up. The delicacy of the
features, the special charm of the woman, suffers more
from these subterfuges which easily become too obvious.
Moreover, man has at his service adjuncts like beard and
moustache which facilitate his task and enable him
frequently to achieve rapid harmony with the part he is
to interpret.

Apart from rouge, the employment of which " effemin-
ates ", masculine make-up is based on the same principles
as feminine make-up. It is more sustained, sometimes
more marked, but does not require as much skill and
experience ; for, as we have said before, the rôle of
the man is not exclusively to please. I would go so far
as to add that in the majority of modern or classical
plays male parts have almost always as their chief or
secondary aim the bringing out of that primordial virtue
of woman, which is to please always and everywhere.

Hints on the Voice

I HAVE said and will repeat that all the formulæ and all the teachers of elocution or of deportment can render very little assistance to the actor who is dreaming of glory. All the instruction that the Conservatoire can impart goes for nothing if the actor is devoid of brain and heart. He may be able to strut about the stage becomingly, or perform graceful evolutions, or enunciate with precision : no doubt. But the favour of the public will turn aside from him after a few bursts of applause.

To forget one's personality and live the part, with real tears and laughter, to link even the breathing of the attentive crowd to the inflexions of one's own emotions —this is what is required. And this cannot be taught.

I will not, however, go so far as to say that to speak anyhow is a matter of indifference, and that the public will find this style of utterance more natural and modern. On the contrary, it is necessary to have an excellent articulation, and many exercises have been recommended to achieve this object.

The same remark applies to the pitch of the voice and breathing, upon which depend the perfect audibility of the voice and the modulation of sentences. But what I must once more emphasize is just this : when on the stage, the actor must forget that he knows how to articulate and how to breathe. He is no longer Mr. This who personates King Lear, nor is the actress Madame That who plays Esther. He *is* King Lear and she *is* Esther. All his knowledge must be implicit in his subconscious mind, that sure and vigilant witness who controls action according to pre-established laws, but never appears and always remains mute and modest.

The voice is produced by the vocal chords, but it undergoes modifications from the successive resonances of the throat, of the mouth, and of the nose. If the mouth and nose did not intervene, or intervened very slightly, the voice would appear to issue from the throat. If the mouth played a preponderant part, it would seem that the voice issued either from the palate or from the teeth.

Now it is undeniable that if the voice, after striking the roof of the mouth, recoils upon the teeth, it is fresher, more malleable, more sonorous ; it does not tremble, it more easily becomes homogeneous and carries better. It has got the right pitch.

It can easily be seen that this pitch of the voice promotes and preserves the clearness of its timbre. The strain is lessened on the throat, which merely lets the sound produced by the vocal chords pass through the windpipe. As the throat does not contract, it does not diminish the purity of the voice. The absence of contraction prevents that congestion of the vocal chords which is the cause of huskiness.

Beginners must therefore make every effort to keep their voices at the right pitch. It is almost impossible to recommend any infallible exercises which would achieve this purpose. The best method is that of example. The pupil should study the posture of the lips and the different muscles of the face and of the neck that come into play when the teacher utters a sound, and he must try to reproduce the same sound by employing his own muscles and opening his mouth in an identical manner. Nevertheless, a certain device which naturally induces a good pitch of the voice may be recommended to the beginner. It consists in addressing oneself to an imaginary auditor placed some distance away. If this point be removed to a sufficient distance, and if the pupil, instead of fixing his attention upon the sounds he is making, will fix it upon this imaginary auditor who is supposed to be hearing everything, throat, mouth, jaw, and lips will instinctively fall into the position required.

The primary sounds produced by the vocal chords are vowels. Consonants are sounds modified by the mouth and various parts of the nasal apparatus ; they have scarcely any influence upon the pitch of the voice.

But what is important to watch is the position of the voice when vowel sounds are produced. In French, O and especially A are throat sounds, while I is sounded with the teeth and the lips. An exercise may be recommended which consists in pronouncing the vowel I in a long breath, keeping the sound steady and regular, and then, without taking fresh breath and preserving the same tone and sound through the teeth, gradually changing the I into E, then into U, into O, and finally into A.

In my opinion no exercises are more useful for voice production than those I have just described.

The problem of breathing is closely connected with that of the pitch of the voice. To know how to breathe is perhaps the most difficult sense to acquire. When young actors and actresses have a long period of words to declaim to the public, they fill their lungs with all the air they can contain, and allow all their breath to escape with the first sentence ; the necessity to take breath again obliges them to hiccough, and they finish in a painful rattle the tirade they had so bravely begun. The vocal chords distend and become inflamed, and gradually the voice becomes husky, and sometimes completely muffled. The voice must be supported by the breath, and the latter must escape gently, flowing with the words. Just as a swimmer inhales a large supply of air before diving, so an actor must inhale a large provision of air before speaking.

There is no occasion to employ bizarre or ridiculous subterfuges, to lay prone and to breathe with a weight on the stomach or on the chest, or to open and shut an umbrella in time with the rhythm of respiration. Such things are the "infallible tricks" of professional charlatans. It is enough to allot oneself the task of pronouncing a certain number of lines in one breath, and to increase this number progressively until the object is attained without strain. By this means the actor will become master of his breathing apparatus, and be able to place it at the service of the passion that must inevitably inform all declamation. If he is liable to stage fright, and should find himself short of breath, he will not hesitate to break off a sentence or even a word in order to take another deep breath.

And better still, the actor will succeed in controlling his nerves and his heart, and in this way counteracting the much feared stage fright itself.

When the beginner is sure of his voice and of his breathing, he may think about articulation, which is only the habit of being precise in the details of pronunciation and of delivery. I can still recall the advice of my godfather when I was preparing for my entrance examination at the Conservatoire. I used to clench my teeth, I did not open the mouth enough for the O, and did not roll my R sufficiently. Here are the hints that are supposed to remedy these defects :

Every morning instead of *do* . . . *re* . . . *mi* practise *te* . . . *de* . . . de in order to learn to vibrate.

Before breakfast repeat forty times : *Un très gros rat dans un très gros trou* : in order to roll the *rs.*

Before dinner repeat forty times : *Combien ces six saucisses-ci ? C'est six sous ces six saucisses-ci ? Six sous ces six saucisses-ci ? Six sous ceux-ci. Six sous ceux-là. Six sous ces six saucisses-ci.* This is to avoid sibilation.

Before going to bed, twenty times : *Didon dina, dit-on, du dos d'un dodu, dindon.* And twenty times : *Le plus petit papa, petit pipi, petit popo, petit pupu.* Open the mouth square for the *d* and pout for the *p.*

There are perhaps better exercises than those of my poor godfather, although they were not very bad (they were harmless enough and without much effect, but sounded very absurd in the toothless mouth of my dear governess Mlle. de Brabender). I would like to quote the exercise which the great artist Lucien Guitry used to set his pupils. Hold a pencil tightly between the teeth, and say the following sentences very quickly and very distinctly :

Roi Paragarapharamus, quand vous désoriginaliserez-vous ? Je me désoriginaliserai quand le plus original des originaux se sera désoriginalisé. Or comme le plus original des originaux ne se désoriginalisera jamais, Paragarapharamus ne se désoriginalisera jamais.

Here is another exercise to practise in the same way :

Petit pot de beurre, quand te dépetit-pot-de-beurreriseras-tu ? Je me dépetit-pot-de-beurreriserai quand tous tous les petits pots de beurre se seront de-petit-pot-beurrerisés.

And another :

Petit grain d'orge, quand te dépetit-grain-d'orgeriseras-tu ? Je me dépetit-grain-d'orgeriserai quand tous les petits grains d'orge se seront dé-petit-grain-d'orgerisés.

Here are two excellent English exercises to practise in the same way :

Sister Susie's sewing shirts for soldiers, sewing shirts for soldiers is all that Sister Susie sews : the soldiers write epistles that they'd sooner sleep on thistles than on the soft shirts that sister Susie sews.

The second :

She sells sea shells on the sea shore and the shells she sells are sea shells I'm sure.

Doubtless one could go on repeating exercises of this kind. All of them are useful and impart a flexibility to the pronunciation that will triumph over all obstacles. The beginner should choose the specimen that contains the obstacles which present most difficulty to him : S. R. P. B. T. D. etc. When he has overcome these obstacles, correcting his defects in the process, he need not concern himself about anything else than the intonation of the sentences and the modulation of verse. It is no longer a question of physical labour or the giving of recipes. The work is purely intellectual, and yet must be given outward expression.

Here is a striking word that lights up everything in a flash. There a word which melts one to tears. If one masters the ideas of the author, and is sure of one's own ideas, then one holds the thread of Ariadne. For the rest, live intensely the life offered you by the poet, with its joys and its sorrows. But I think I have already said all I have to say on this subject. And my own career is the best and latest example that I can give in this little book.